BARRIER-
free
FRIENDSHIPS

Other books by Joni Eareckson Tada

All God's Children

Diamonds in the Dust

Heaven: Your Real Home

Joni: An Unforgettable Story

The Life and Death Dilemma:
Suicide, Euthanasia, Suffering, Mercy

**A COMPLETELY REVISED AND UPDATED
EDITION OF *FRIENDSHIP UNLIMITED***

BARRIER-
Free
FRIENDSHIPS

BRIDGING THE DISTANCE BETWEEN
YOU AND FRIENDS WITH DISABILITIES

JONI EARECKSON TADA
AND STEVE JENSEN

ZondervanPublishingHouse
Grand Rapids, Michigan

A Division of HarperCollinsPublishers

Barrier-Free Friendships
Copyright © 1997 by Joni Eareckson Tada

Previously published as *Friendship Unlimited,* now revised and updated

Requests for information should be addressed to:

🏛ZondervanPublishingHouse
Grand Rapids, Michigan 49530

Library of Congress Cataloging-in-Publication Data

Tada, Joni Eareckson.
    Barrier-free friendships: bridging the distance between you and friends with
disabilities / Joni Eareckson Tada and Steve Jensen.
        p. cm.
    Rev. Ed. of: Friendship unlimited / by Joni Eareckson Tada with Bev
Singleton. 1987.
    Includes bibliographical references.
    ISBN: 0-310-21007-0 (pbk.)
    1. Handicapped—United States—Psychology.   2. Handicapped—Care—
United States.   3. Helping behavior.   4. Handicapped—Religious life.   I.
Jensen, Steve.   II. Tada, Joni Eareckson.   Friendship unlimited.   III. Title.
HV1553.T33   1997
362.4'048—dc21   96-49114
                                                                                CIP

Published in association with Wolgemuth & Hyatt, Incorporated, 8012 Brooks
Chapel Road, #243, Brentwood, Tennessee 37027.

Interior design by Sherri Hoffman

Printed in the United States of America

---

97 98 99 00 01 02 03 04 /❖ DH/ 10 9 8 7 6 5 4 3 2 1

Contents

To John Wern, a friend's friend.

Part One

In Search of a Friend

ONE

Where Can I Find a Friend?

I̲T WAS A HIT-AND-RUN waiting to happen.

Tracy, a young woman with two preschoolers, roamed the department store, hoping to find something to fit both her budget and her image of herself before she and her husband had a third child. Though she loved her husband and her children, she longed for something she had not yet found. Shopping, cooking, and a part-time job left her little time for herself. She felt overwhelmed at times; sometimes she even felt as though she lived in a cage.

I need a break, Tracy told herself as she strolled through the misses sizes. *And an adult to talk to.* Tracy thought back to those days in high school when she would hang out with her friends and dream about boys they would marry and the trips they would take around the world. The freedom in those friendships had enabled her to dream. And that is what she missed, more than the dreams themselves. Her daydream caused her not to notice her three-year-old diving into the center of a rack of coats.

At the same moment, Lana, a single woman disabled by cerebral palsy, wheeled through the aisles of blouses and sweaters. She seldom shopped alone because it was difficult to get to the store. The residential facility where she lived offered only sporadic field trips to the mall, and even when a van was available, the cost was usually more than what Lana had left over from the monthly state stipend of thirty-five dollars.

The rare occasion that Lana did go shopping was usually a painful experience. When she tried to communicate with the clerks, they would either ignore her or give up trying to understand her questions. Sometimes Lana left with the wrong size because it was easier to pull something off the nearest shelf in the hope that it would fit or look nice. Or she would return home without having purchased anything at all.

On the day of the incident, Lana had promised herself this trip would be different. *I'm not going to leave without the blouse I really want,* she told herself. *No matter what it takes.*

For years Lana had lived in a world where people dictated her schedule and defined her limits. Her friends were of the medical and professional variety: a therapist to hold her while she walked the parallel bars; an attendant to help her bathe; a speech therapist to get her to talk clearly; a social worker to file the latest batch of papers with the state. They were all pleasant people, but none touched the real Lana—the Lana inside.

Kids stared at her. Strangers remained just that, parting themselves to make room for her to steer her wheelchair through. The more compassionate would sometimes step in and help but would never linger for conversation. Eye contact was limited to glances. She had long ago given up hope that the glances would change to genuine smiles, that a helper would become a friend. Like a caged lion, she accepted the bars that kept her from such relationships. She too lived in a cage.

Then it happened. Tracy's child leaped out of the coats just as Lana passed by in her wheelchair. Lana jerked back in surprise, her body thrashing in uncontrolled spasms. Her foot pushed against the floor, sending her wheelchair in reverse and knocking over the display of mannequins. Plastic arms, legs, and heads crashed down around Lana. She froze in terror and embarrassment. Her hands covered her head as if she were waiting for someone to strike her.

Tracy heard the crash and turned in time to see the last mannequin limb hit the ground. She ran to rescue the victims. A surge of emotions gripped her. Anger at her child for being involved. Embarrassment that she would be blamed for the mishap. And then fear that she wouldn't know how to handle the huddled shape she saw in the wheelchair. *What do I do?* she thought.

Lana peered out from under her arms. Before her stood the three-year-old. Behind him, the mother, looking confused and flustered.

"Are you okay?" Tracy whispered.

Lana nodded jerkily.

"I'm so sorry. Here, Michael," she said to her son, "you pick up the pieces and put them on the stand." The child did not move but rather stared at Lana. "C'mon honey. Help me," Tracy tugged at Michael's arm while she began picking up parts. Lana stared back at the child. She worked to say something, but Tracy's insistence with Michael cut her off.

The store clerk had come to the scene by this time. "Don't worry folks," she said to Tracy. "We'll clean up here. You continue shopping with your friend."

"Oh, she's not . . ." Tracy stopped mid-sentence, afraid the words might hurt the disabled woman's feelings. Lana looked up at Tracy, acknowledging the attempt with a weak smile.

"Mommy, what's wrong with the lady?" Michael asked.

"Nothing, honey. She's just . . ." Tracy didn't know how to answer. She wanted to get out of there as soon as possible.

"I'm disabled," Lana worked to say. "Ammm dish-shay-booled" is what came out. The boy stood back a little and stared at the jaws that were clenched in a big grin. He clung to his mother's legs.

"I'm really sorry," Tracy said. "Michael's never met anyone who's crippled before." *Neither have I,* thought Tracy. "Well, I guess we'll keep shopping. Are you okay?"

Lana nodded, wanting to say more and hoping the accident would somehow linger. But she could see that a restless baby in Tracy's walker and a rambunctious boy and a mom on a mission could not be held captive to her need for finding a blouse. And her need to find a friend.

Tracy looked at Lana. She wondered how the woman got there. Wondered if she understood much. Wondered what Lana thought of her. Tracy looked into Lana's eyes and thought she saw a glimmer of something she remembered from long ago. But seeing the jerky motions of Lana's body, the wheelchair, the strained attempts at talking, Tracy knew Lana was part of a different world. Tracy went on her way.

Nothing I can do here, she thought. *I've got to keep shopping and then get home to clean and then to McDonalds....* And then maybe to find a friend somewhere.

Lana made her way to the van without a purchase. Tracy walked through the aisles on her search, her face flushed hot in embarrassment for quite some time. The women never saw each other again—two caged hearts in search of a friendship that could have made all the difference to them. And all the difference to the world around them.

A Call for Friendship

LANA'S AND TRACY'S STORY is often rehearsed in our world between all kinds of people, not just between those who are able or disabled. Our society is marked by alienation. We "cocoon" in our homes, in our personal computers, in our televisions. The ease with which people move from place to place makes us cautious in our relationships, and the commodity of trust seems to be in short supply.

Against such a backdrop, how could a book like this ever lead people to make friends with a disabled person? Fostering any kind of friendship is hard, let alone with a person who seems different. Why take on the impossible task of bridging such different worlds?

First, the worlds aren't as different as we imagine. Oh, yes, my life is different because of my disability and things like pressure sores, catheters, and corsets that wear wounds on my hips. Then there are the obvious emotions involving deep and permanent loss. But the basic issues of life are the same with me as they are with you. I need love and a sense of security. I wonder about my place in this world. I have tastes and opinions. I battle the flesh and sometimes wish that I was better, faster, kinder, smarter, prettier, and younger. And I want heaven to be here now.

Second, God wants to see the people in these worlds joined together. As you will discover in a later chapter, Jesus Christ lived and breathed friendship, especially friendships with people with disabilities. This book isn't based on my vision for the 549 million disabled people in this world who need a friend. It is based on Jesus' burning passion to see his people reach everyone in the world for whom he died. His passion burns especially hot for those the world counts as weak.

Third, the people in these seemingly different worlds have so much to offer each other. I have met scores of people, disabled and nondisabled, who have found in each other true friendship. The people involved, and their families, have had their lives changed for the better because of such friendships.

This last point needs more explanation if you are to continue reading this book. You probably selected this book because you "have a heart." You want to "minister." You want to "help." Great! You're A1 in my book.

But consider what's in it for *you!* Sounds a bit worldly to be basing your friendship on a self-centered view, doesn't it? But don't forget that God promised us blessings if we love as he commanded us to love. Consider the direct promise described by Jesus in Luke 14:13–14 when we extend our friendship to people with disabilities. He said that we would be repaid at the resurrection of the righteous when we extend friendship to people with disabilities. I can't imagine how God will repay, but his smallest payback exceeds our greatest sacrifice in eternal proportions.

Beyond that future promise, there are blessings for today when we love others. Love, expressed in friendship, includes in its biblical description the idea of personal gain. John Piper's book *Desiring God* has a wonderful chapter on this idea. He says that we often overlook this aspect of love when we read 1 Corinthians 13. Paul says, "If I give all I possess to the poor and surrender my body to the flames, but have not love, *I gain nothing*" (italics mine). What a curious statement to make. Could there be a gain to something as selfless as love?

Consider Paul's words to the Ephesians, "It is more blessed to give than to receive." We assume blessed means "good," or "right." Actually, it means "happy" or "joyous"—benefiting the *giver.* Again, how odd that we should entertain—that God should entertain—the notion that there is something for us in the transaction of love. Friendships have love at their core. And initiating friendships with people with disabilities is likewise an initiation of love. There is benefit for the recipient. There is benefit for the giver.

What blessings will you find in befriending a disabled person? Each friendship has its unique joys, but let me share several I have found to be common to many relationships between disabled and nondisabled people.

You will find someone with whom to share your struggles

Not every disabled person qualifies as a marriage-and-family counselor, nor are they the sweet, ever patient Corrie-ten-

Boom-like grandmother. But many are more than willing to listen. Don't assume that a disabled person only thinks about ramps, Medicaid, and if the handicap stalls in the bathrooms are wide enough. And please don't think that every disabled person is desperate to have someone—anyone—pay a tad of attention to their needs. Perhaps the greatest asset that most disabled people possess is patience. We have had scads of time—whether waiting in line or waiting to get up in the morning—to cultivate the art of sitting and listening.

Disabled people *can* relate. Second Corinthians 1:4 reminds us that "we can comfort those in any trouble with the comfort we ourselves have received from God." Lana in our story may not be able to flash wallet photos of her firstborn, but her struggles in learning endurance and patience have prepared her well to be "all ears" when it comes to Tracy's problems.

You will find someone to remind you of the grace of God

Not every person with a disability is gracious. But the message disabled people underscore just by "being" is that God is gracious. He is in the miraculous business of sustaining the weak, always drawing us into a deeper dependency upon him. Disabilities in others remind us of this powerful truth.

Friends with disabilities remind us of God's grace in another way. For without Christ, you were once disabled spiritually, unable to move into his kingdom, as well as blind to his purposes and deaf to his voice. But by his grace you are being made whole; and it's the disability in others which serves as God's physical audiovisual aid of how he's working spiritually in the lives of us all.

You will find someone to slow you down

My friends would laugh. "Joni, you're anything but slow. You keep *us* running after *you!*" Touché. But getting a disabled friend from here to there may take longer than you realize. Dressing routines may double preparation time. Walking beside a person with a walker may limit your sightseeing. Explaining something to a mentally disabled person might be frustrating because they don't get it "now."

These may seem to be annoyances at first. But the effect of the slower speed, if accepted, teaches you the value of steadiness and enjoying the journey as much as the destination.

You will find someone to stretch you as a person

You have spent enough time getting comfortable with life. It is time to develop your character, expand your horizons, trust in God's hand beyond your small world. You'll find yourself coping with new problems and solving them together. Self-consciousness will begin to fade as you encounter awkward and sometimes humorous situations. You should hear the stories of friends who have gotten themselves into scrapes with department stores and airlines.

One friend had braved a revolving door of a store with her friend in a wheelchair. "We won't make it," Donna had said from her place in the chair. "We'll make it," Cheryl had said. They didn't. Cheryl could get Donna in, but as the door and the chair made its arc, they found that the chair was angled in such a way as to get it stuck about three-fourths of the way in. A couple of hours later, Donna was unstuck and the two were on their way, laughing for years to come about their adventure.

A Godly Desire

SOME OF YOU MAY still view such self-centered reasons as somehow tainting the friendship. But consider the person with a disability for a moment and how they would feel if you held to a sense of duty as a basis for your friendship. They have enough dutiful people in their lives that have taken them on as a "mission" of love. How will they know if you really love them and whether or not they are really valued if you do not seek out a relationship based on your desire?

Are you ready to discover a new joy?

TWO

Making a Difference in Spite of Barriers

REMEMBER IN ELEMENTARY SCHOOL when a big argument would erupt between a couple of kids? You would arrive on the scene amid yelling and name calling. If boys were involved, some shoving and wrestling might ensue. It would usually end when a teacher stepped in, and more often than not, the teacher's first question would be, "All right, who started this?"

Impossible question, really. And of course, the individuals involved usually pointed at each other. Since neither side seemed totally innocent, the teacher usually punished both of them. "I don't care who started it, fighting's wrong. You're both to blame." It was a tidy answer but each kid knew the truth, I'm sure. One of them *had* started it.

So it is with friendships. Projecting back to the start of a relationship is difficult, but if we could "replay the videotape," we would see that someone did start it. We don't live in a world where personalities and circumstances mix at random to create relationships. Someone has to start the ball rolling. Whether it was a simple smile that made a train ride a pleasure for two strangers who would never see each other again or whether it was a word of trust spoken in crisis to spawn a lifelong friendship, someone had to take the initiative for relationships to begin.

It is no different for people with disabilities. When it comes to relationships with members of this community, I ask that those of you who are not disabled take the initiative. You need to take the risk of looking past the wheelchair, the sunglasses, and the prostheses to see and engage the person that lies hidden there.

I have no doubt raised a few eyebrows with that request. I sound like someone who believes disabled people are unable to carry out meaningful relationships, let alone a conversation. Quite the contrary, I know that many people with disabilities have great interpersonal skills and initiate wonderful relationships.

But thirty years of moving in this wheelchair among pews, rehab centers, dirt villages, and government buildings has taught me that people with disabilities often get set aside. In some cases they have become an oppressed minority. They have had to adjust to a world system that is not designed with them in mind. Laws, cultural norms, business transactions, and underlying attitudes can make them feel like second class citizens. If you have a disability, taking the initiative in such an environment can be difficult and risky.

Why? Well, consider what John Powell observes about relationships in his book *Why Am I Afraid to Tell You Who I Am?* He writes, "I am afraid to tell you who I am, because if I tell you who I am, you may not like who I am, and it's all that I have."

"You may not like who I am!" That observation gets to the heart of one of the difficulties that a disabled person has in initiating relationships. People with disabilities can't hide their reasons for rejection. In most cases they are plainly visible. "I am weak," the crutches seem to say. "I can't see," the white cane announces. "I'm different," the face of the Down syndrome teen states. These unspoken statements are usually cause for rejection in our society where abilities, intelligence, and good looks are highly prized.

Fear of rejection is not some theoretical problem. I can relate to that from personal experience. I remember the days in the rehab hospital wondering how my friends from high school would accept me. I was the same person I was before on the inside, but my props had been taken away. No more horses, no more field hockey, no more dates on a Friday night. I wondered, *Will they still accept me? Or will they find reasons to reject me?*

Fear of rejection is only a part of what makes it difficult for a disabled person to initiate relationships. Barriers exist everywhere that require enormous energy to overcome. Think about what it takes to be someone's friend. Rather than being a casual activity, you will find that you invest resources in that friendship. Time, energy, and finances "lubricate" the process. You will also find that people's perception of you also can facilitate your relationships. The more social "assets" you have, the greater the ease with which you are able to enter into friendships.

People with disabilities find barriers with regard to these issues. To be a friend to people with disabilities, it is important for you to understand what these barriers are. It will not only motivate you to take the initiative, it will also guide you in how to take the initiative. Please be assured that not every person with a disability faces all of these barriers all of the time. This is a composite picture. But just one barrier would make it difficult to spend the energy to initiate and maintain a friendship.

A Community in Crisis

DAY-TO-DAY LIFE FOR A person with a disability can be a major ordeal. Employment, family life, housing, transportation, and medical needs can consume a disabled person. The time and energy and money needed to cope in these arenas can greatly inhibit one's ability to enter into relationships with people.

Unemployment is approximately 63 percent in our country for people with disabilities. In some countries, it is nearly 100 percent. In a world that values work so highly, to be unemployed carries a stigma. You run the risk of being considered an unproductive member of society. Having a job also places you in the company of others on a regular basis. The job site becomes a fruitful place to develop friendships. And having a job means having the freedom to make economic decisions like, "Do I have enough money to go out for pizza tonight with my friends?" or "Can I afford the cost of transportation to go to the mall?"

As important as employment might be, it doesn't guarantee viable friendships. The strain of a disability on family life can create enormous obstacles. Physical strength can be drained of energy in caring for a disabled member. The sheer weight of loss—loss of dreams, affections, income, relationship—can crush the family structure.

"You never have time for me, anymore."

"I'm not your nurse, I'm your wife."

"We can't ever take a vacation because of Billy."

"We never go out with other couples anymore."

In some cases, the strain becomes too much to bear. Divorce is often the only option available for people. Sadly, the divorce rate in our country is approximately 80 percent for those with a disabled member in the family! The divorce can send the member with a disability down the path of guilt, shame, and loneliness. The young disabled child loses Mom and Dad and blames himself and his disability for the breakup. The disabled spouse, desperately in need of the other as a lover, provider, and friend, finds himself or herself the object of scorn or irritation. They have no other explanation for the cause of the breakup other than the disability. Such feelings serve as further obstacles in a person's attempt to create healthy friendships.

Compounding unemployment and divorce is the matter of finding suitable housing, which doesn't just happen by opening up the classified ads. Disabled people may need clear access in and around the home. They may not be able to live on their own due to medical reasons. Or they simply may not be able to afford independent living. Suitable housing for people with some types of disabilities is sometimes unavailable.

Finding suitable housing can be a major ordeal, but getting to work, to church, or to the doctor's office can be just as frustrating. Public transportation is often erratic, if it is available at all. Because so many relationships depend upon meeting people in social contexts, difficulties in transportation can pose a major barrier for people with disabilities.

Medical issues can be no less worrisome. A person with a disability is not by definition "sick," but boy can my body consume me! When you become disabled, you are initiated into a club where your body becomes more expensive to maintain than a luxury automobile. In thirty years I have spent over 43,800 hours in the hospital or in bed from pressure sores, tens of thousands of dollars in medically related expenses, and 262,000 hours going through daily care routines! Medical issues absorb time, energy, and money that could otherwise be invested in relationships.

All such day-to-day issues can inhibit a person with a disability from seeking out friendships, even deeply desired friendships. Yet those who have successfully dealt with the life issues I have discussed have been those who have found friends to assist them. Rehab counselors and advocacy groups are wisely encouraging people with disabilities to face life's challenges by putting together a team of friends. Some disabled people are catching the vision. Others are not. But friendships for persons with disabilities remain in short supply.

A World of Labels

A WOMAN RECENTLY WROTE me about her daughter who has Down syndrome. She mentioned that she and her husband have become keenly sensitive to the experiences of the disabled. Then she edited herself and suggested the word "handicapped." Then, as if holding a red pencil, she made one more change. She scribbled in a bunch of question marks as if to say she wasn't certain what word to use. In frustration, I pictured her throwing her hands up in the air. The woman lamented that she didn't know which word was least likely to be read as a derogatory label.

I can appreciate this mother's predicament. Nobody wants to purposefully stick a label on another. The labels "disabled," "handicapped," "special," or even "challenged" can box a person into certain categories. Labels such as these are often associated with weakness and dependency. No matter how strong or independent the person might be, a label speaks volumes. Labels can limit people and foster negative impressions. They segregate ... separate.

People with disabilities, no matter how sociable, will often find a label attached to them. Even well-intentioned actions can perpetuate the idea that disabled people are different. For example, you've probably seen handicapped entrances at amusement parks. People with disabilities will be escorted to the entrance. As they take their place in line, you have already placed them in a category. They are getting "special" treatment reserved for "people like them" who "need help" because they "can't function like everyone else."

It is a subtle message we communicate, but do you see how even an extremely gifted and intelligent disabled person could be labeled as weak and dependent, simply by getting a reserved spot in line? Now I'm not suggesting I give up my parking space at the restaurant! Please, that would be a disaster. But I am saying it's difficult to disassociate my parking space from an emotional response on your part. I am labeled simply because of the sign above the space and the ideas associated with that sign.

A Jungle of Emotions

DAILY CRISES AND NEGATIVE labels aren't the only things that make life difficult for people with disabilities. What happens in the minds of people without disabilities can make it almost impossible.

According to a Harris poll done in 1991, 57 percent of people without disabilities felt uncomfortable with disabled people. Such discomfort can stem from a person's reaction to the appearance of the disabled person—a wheelchair, different facial features, or a missing limb. Or a disabled person's behavior or speech pattern might elicit discomfort. Do you remember the first time you visited the hospital or the nursing home? If you're like most people, it gave you a queasy feeling, and you weren't sure you wanted to be there. The environment was different. You didn't know what to expect.

Discomfort with people with disabilities might also be accompanied by fear. In the same Harris survey, 47 percent polled felt *afraid* of disabled people. What are they afraid of? Some might be afraid of being embarrassed, I suppose. I have met so many nervous people who simply didn't know how to say hello. They thought they would say or do something foolish. One research study I heard indicated that a basic fear that people have is that they will catch the disability themselves. It is news to some people that you can't catch cerebral palsy any more than you could catch brown hair!

How would you feel if you created discomfort or fear in people? Would you be excited about initiating friendships? Probably not. You would wonder if the person sitting next to you at the Laundromat was looking for an excuse to get away from you as quickly as possible. Or you might assume that even if someone was cordial enough to talk with you, he or she really wanted to do something else. That is why I encourage you to be the one to take the initiative, showing that you aren't afraid or uncomfortable.

It Makes a Difference

BUT DOES IT MAKE a difference to initiate a friendship? Even a friendly acquaintance? Yes, it does. Let me illustrate what it meant for friends to take the initiative in my life. I faced a multitude of problems, many like the ones just described. I was in the rehab ward when the process began.

"How can Joni best be helped?" my parents had asked the doctor after I got settled into my new room.

I listened as the man in the white coat and my mother and father stood at the base of my bed and talked. The doctor flipped through a chart and began the speech he had given time and time before.

I was suddenly assaulted by a barrage of new words, foreign and frightful. I was a severely involved quadriplegic with a transversal spinal lesion sustained at the fractured fourth/fifth cervical level. I would be fitted with an in-dwelling foley catheter and be given seven pills daily. I would have two hours of physical therapy a day. I was to spend time in occupational therapy. Once a week I was to go to the office of my vocational rehabilitation counselor, and twice a week to a peer-group counseling session. Every kind of specialist was assigned to me—a urologist, psychologist, internist, a pulmonary specialist, and every other "ist" imaginable.

Whew!

After the doctor left, I asked someone to pull the sheet over my head and turn on the television to crowd out my frightful feelings. I peeked out from under the sheet at my roommates. One girl in a wheelchair puffed on a cigarette and stared aimlessly out the window of our ward. Another girl cracked gum and filed her nails, waiting by her food tray. Another girl, paralyzed and blind, lay in bed, her unfocused gaze fixed on the ceiling.

"Hi," I said to the girl filing her nails. "How long have you been here?"

She squinted at the ceiling, thinking. "Oh, I guess going on two years," she said matter-of-factly.

Two years! I turned my head the other way and fought back tears. This was my first day of rehab and I was already lonely. It was a world that I was neither comfortable nor acquainted with. And this was only the beginning.

Insecure and intimidated, I managed to learn the "buzz words" that seemed to be second nature to the guys in wheelchairs who hung around the elevator. Yet every time I was wheeled past them on my way to physical therapy I could barely look them in the eyes and muster a smile.

I felt the same way whenever I passed by one of the older women strapped in her wheelchair, parked by the wall. Will that be me someday?

I bit my lip, resolved and rigid. No. I could not ... would not ... believe that a successful rehabilitation would depend solely on the rehab center, its routines, and health care professionals. These people—doctors, nurses, and therapists—would surely play a profound role in helping me toward independence and acceptance.

But there had to be more.

So ... Who Helped the Most?

WHAT WAS THE ONE thing I needed the most? Friends!

A few of those friends were merely acquaintances—nurses from other wards who would occasionally stop by to check in and say hi. Other friends were casual—students who stopped by for an occasional visit between classes at a nearby college.

Some friends became close—people who visited regularly, shared common interests and visions, and helped me see beyond the hospital walls into a world that was waiting outside. Still others grew to be intimate friends—people who went with me to therapy or became my advocate with the nursing supervisor, always going the second mile, giving their coat when I asked for their shirt.

I could now easily answer the question my parents posed to that doctor the first afternoon at rehab. Friends—acquaintances, casual, close, or even intimate—made all the difference in the world.

And if I were to pinpoint the one common denominator these friends shared, it would be love. Love strong enough to overcome the stale, stuffy smell in my hospital room. Love strong enough to break through the fear of "having nothing to talk about." Love that refused to be squeamish when they had to empty my leg bag. And love that saw potential in me, even though I was reduced to doing not much more than writing with a pen between my teeth.

Let me share with you an example of someone who initiated a relationship with me. Some time later a friend—an older man who was an extremely skilled artist—came often to challenge and inspire me through those early days of learning how not only write but to paint while holding a brush between my teeth. He would bring in old books from his library, new kinds of paint, or different and unusual brushes.

At first I thought surely he had better things to do. Wasn't there someone more important he should be spending his time with? But he kept coming to see me.

His talent began to catch my interest. Some of the brushes he showed me were more than thirty years old—and they looked every day of it. The paint on the handles was chipped and discolored. The bristles were stubbly and uneven. If I hadn't known better, I would have said his brushes were useless, not fit for painting anything of real value.

One afternoon while giving my jaw a rest from clenching my brush, I watched him work in front of his easel. Miraculously, in his hands the brushes became not only useful, but priceless. He swirled and swept the paint on his canvas. Each of those ugly brushes had its own purpose: one was for broad, thick strokes, another was for thin, straight lines.

Sitting there mesmerized, I noticed that he avoided using the new, soft sable brushes from the occupational therapy department. This artist friend of mine preferred to work with his well-worn, well-proven tools. And my friend knew his tools well. He knew what each brush could and could not do in his hands.

As a beautiful painting began to take shape on his canvas, a saying I had often heard before came to mind: A tool unto itself is of little importance, but placed in the proper hands it can create a masterpiece.

My gaze dropped to my paralyzed legs. It struck me that God wanted to do a similar work in my life.

Behind those institutional walls for too many months, I had begun to feel of little use and almost no value, like a worn-out ugly thing of inferior quality and little worth. Even though that same institution did its best to help me, the rules and mechanical, day-to-day routines had barely made a crack in my tough exterior of calloused depression.

Oh sure, it was good to see some progress at physical therapy. Being able to sit up in a wheelchair for five hours was a major achievement. And yes, it was helpful to make those first, shaky attempts at feeding myself in occupational therapy. The peer counseling sessions, closely monitored by a watchful professional, benefited me some. And even my vocational rehabilitation counselor helped me open my eyes slightly to future possibilities of college and employment. But that dear elderly man did for me what all the routines of rehabilitation could not. He gave me love—warm and personal, compassionate and accepting. Under his kind instruction I began to practice with perseverance, believing that I could actually paint as well as he said I could!

Becoming a Masterpiece

LOOKING BACK, I WISH I could put myself in the shoes of that elderly man. Perhaps at first he thought that I was not fit for anything great in the kingdom of God. After all, I could do little more than clumsily slop paint on a plaster of Paris candy dish. He may have thought I was for the most part useless, having no real value to accomplish anything wonderful for the Lord. Maybe he could have assumed I had gone through too much—a rebellious period, an angry, teenaged stubbornness—to look past the depressing present to the hopeful future.

But I believe my artist friend knew a precious secret, a secret that will be passed on to you in this little book. It is this: weak and seemingly inferior people may seem to lack importance, but placed in the hands of the Master they can be a masterpiece.

The apostle Paul nearly said the same when he wrote in 2 Corinthians 4:7–12,

> This priceless treasure we hold, so to speak, in a common earthenware jar—to show that the splendid power of it belongs to God and not to us. We are handicapped on all sides, but we are never frustrated; we are puzzled, but never in despair. . . . Every day we experience something of the death of the Lord Jesus, so that we may also know the power of the life of Jesus in these bodies of ours. (PHILLIPS).

Through the love and acceptance that my artist friend showed me I too experienced the power of God. He walked into my room as a mere acquaintance. But over the months we became close. And now I would count him as a dear and intimate friend. The Lord used him to bring me out of despair and feelings of rejection. I hadn't asked him to do that. He took the risk, stepped across the barriers I had created, and released my love for art.

And for life.

THREE

A True Friend Identifies

H AVE YOU EVER WATCHED a football game and seen those crazy fans in the stands wearing face paint and funny hats, braving temperatures well below zero? They scream at the top of their lungs to cheer for their team, as if the players will actually listen to their instructions. And put them in front of a TV camera and you would think they had just won the lottery! If you are watching the game at home, you say to yourself, "Why do they do that?"

The answer isn't found in the win-loss record of the team. In baseball, for example, some of the most avid fans are Cub fans whose team hasn't won the pennant in eighty years! The answer lies not in the team itself but in the heart of the true fan.

What the crazy fans in the stadium, as well as the more subdued fans in the living room (like my husband, Ken, and I!), experience in our heart is called *identification*. We identify with the team. Our identity as individuals is tied, even in a small way, to the team. As a resident of the Los Angeles area, the Lakers are a part of me and I feel like a part of them. If they win, we're happy. If they lose, we're sad. (Ken more than me!) And we will defend the honor of the team to any who would disparage it.

A true fan will recount stories of past triumphs. Or quote statistics on the players. Or wear jackets, hats, pins, and shirts with the team's logo, when they are playing and in the off-season. A true fan will do this because he or she identifies with the team. Wouldn't it be wonderful if we identified with one another as people in the same way? Someone's hurt becomes my hurt? Someone's hope becomes my hope?

Nowhere is a sense of identification more needed than in relationships between nondisabled people and disabled people. Whether you simply cross each other's paths briefly or become intimate friends, developing a sense of identification with a disabled person is the most important and rewarding step you can take. To identify with a person with a disability will mean that you have taken yet another step in conforming to the image of Christ.

If identification is that important, let's define it and then describe it in further detail. Webster's dictionary says it is a "process by which a person ascribes to himself the qualities or characteristics of another person." It is also described as "the perception of another person as an extension of oneself" (that is, your pain is my pain; your joy, my joy).

Nobel prize winner Herbert Simon describes identification this way: "We will say that a person identifies himself with a group when, in making a decision, he evaluates the several alternatives of choice in terms of their consequences for the specified group (or person)."

The essence of a friendship with a person with a disability is that we think about choices (how we will act, what we will say) based upon their impact on that person and consider that person to be an extension of ourselves. It means that we will look at the world from their perspective and act accordingly.

Whether or not we identify with someone with a disability will depend upon these two factors: what we know about a person and how well we value that person. Borrowing again from Herbert Simon, these factors are called "premises." We make decisions about things and about people based on premises of what we believe to be true (facts) as well as the things that are important to us or that we care about (values).

To illustrate how we make decisions, imagine for a moment that you're in the market for a car. Your pragmatic nature determines that safety and economy might be important values to you. As you shop for cars, you will base your decision on information related to those values. Miles per gallon, air bags, and antilock brakes will all be key factors in helping you determine which car you buy. (If you choose a convertible sports car, you weren't being honest about what you valued. Looks and speed were probably more important to you!)

When it comes to our attitudes toward other people, we go through a similar process. Because an attitude is simply a decision we make with regard to a person, idea, or thing, our values and the information available to us will be of central interest.

Let us take this line of thinking and illustrate how you can not only describe your attitude toward a person with a disability, but also how you can grow in your relationship with that person or group of people. At the same time, we will see other attitudes that are prevalent in our society today regarding people with disabilities.

First, think about information regarding people with disabilities. You can have varying amounts of accurate or inaccurate information (facts) about someone. Represented in graphic form, it looks like this:

+ Facts

- Facts

Second, think about your value regarding people with disabilities. Your value can move in a positive or negative direction and can be represented this way.

- Value ←——————————→ + Value

Those of you who remember (enjoyed or dreaded!) algebra class can see where I'm going with this. Put the two lines together to form a graph of Facts and Value:

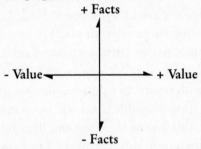

You will notice that when we formed this graph, we created four areas or quadrants. Look at each quadrant to see what's there.

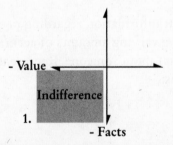

Quadrant 1: Lesser value with little or inaccurate information. This is the quadrant of *Indifference.* "I don't know and I don't care" is how someone with little value and little or inaccurate information would express it. Very few would actually say it that way, but it is prevalent in our society when it comes to

working with disabled people. As a group, disabled people have experienced discrimination and have had to work hard to get the most essential laws passed to protect them from indifference.

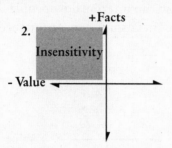

Quadrant 2: Lesser value but with accurate and increasing amount of information.

This is the quadrant of *Insensitivity.* A person may know what is happening with people with disabilities but may not respond positively because he or she doesn't care or has gotten burned out from caring. This often happens with those working professionally in the field of disability. The disabled person may become just another "problem," "case," or "file."

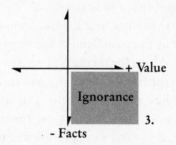

Quadrant 3: Positive value but with inaccurate or inadequate information.

This is the quadrant of *Ignorance.* A lot of people in churches fall into this category. They care a lot—Christ's example and command prompt this—but they simply don't know. They are unaware. That is why much of disability ministry is geared toward building awareness. Ignorance can be expressed in things such as assuming a person who is mentally disabled is also deaf. Or a person in a wheelchair might be assumed to be mentally disabled. You can imagine how people would interact in such cases and why friendships or acquaintances would be so hard to get started.

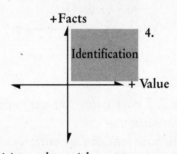

Quadrant 4: Positive value with more, accurate information. This is the quadrant of *Identification.* The more we value a person with a disability and the more we know, the more we will identify with them. Notice that with even a little bit of information and a little bit of value, you have moved away from where many people are in society.

As we move further into the quadrant of Identification, we learn more about a person. And at the same time we grow in our appreciation and love for them. We begin to learn secrets of what is important to them—simple things like their tastes in music and deeper things like their motivations in life. All the while we esteem them more highly and view them more and more as someone created in God's image. We will find creative ways of loving the person and valuing the person the way God values.

We have come full circle in this chapter now. We said at the outset that our goal in friendship is identification. Exciting for each Christian is that if we decide to value and learn as much as we can about a person with a disability, we will have expressed the mind of Christ by identifying with that person. Christ *iden-*

tified with us in the flesh. He became one of us and knows our frame. He valued us enough to die for us.

Imitating Christ in Friendship

THAT IS WHAT THIS is about, isn't it? Imitating Christ who was the ultimate Friend.

Jesus was the Friend of sinners. And his friendship was so strong that he identified with us in his death when he took on our sins and endured the wrath of God. Oh, what an expression of loving friendship to identify so closely with us!

Just as Jesus identified with people in his death, he also identified with us in his life. And in the thirty-three years that Jesus spent on earth, he paid particular attention to what was considered to be a rather unlovely group of people—people with disabilities! Did you know that twenty-five out of the thirty-four miracles recorded in the Gospels are with people with disabilities? On every page you see Jesus interacting with disabled people, befriending them, and meeting them at their point of need!

Jesus' friendship with people with disabilities serves as a model for us. We can't go wrong if we imitate the way in which he identified with people with disabilities. He valued each disabled person as a person. The story of the paralytic who was let down through the roof in Luke 5 highlights Jesus' belief that a disabled person was a *person*. In verse 20, he addresses the man as "friend," or literally "man." That one word cut right through the prevailing notion that disabled people were less than full participants in society.

While elevating the status of each disabled person to that of a true human, Jesus also saw that each disabled person was also a *sinner*. We have a tendency to idealize people with disabilities as somehow incapable of sinning. But Jesus didn't sugarcoat human nature, even when it came to those who might elicit sympathy or pity in our society. In some cases, Jesus pointed out the disabled person's need for forgiveness. The disability may not have been caused by the sin, as in the story of the blind man in John 9, but that did not exclude the person with a disability from the community of sinners. Several times Jesus told disabled people that their sins were forgiven or that they should sin no more.

Jesus not only knew the true nature of a disabled person, he also felt *compassion* for them. Whether dealing with an individual or masses of people with disabilities, the Gospels often say that "he had compassion" on them. He did not ignore the need of the day and trivialize it in light of more important matters like the kingdom. He took each person at their point of need and expressed tender mercy. I like that synonym for compassion: "tender mercy." When we identify with a person with a disability like Christ did, we will be tender in doing so. Whatever harshness or difficulty our disabled friend might throw at us, we can be tender in our response.

Jesus included people with disabilities as a part of his *mission* on earth. When asked in Luke 7 whether or not he was the Messiah, look at how he answered: "Go back and report to John what you have seen and heard: The blind receive sight, the lame walk, those who have leprosy are cured, the deaf hear, the dead are raised, and the good news is preached to the poor." In our "mission" for Jesus, we might have easily skipped over this group. But Jesus didn't forget. And neither should we.

Jesus *stopped to listen* to people with disabilities. The story of Bartimaeus illustrates this characteristic of Jesus. Bartimaeus, while sitting beside the road to Jericho, called out to Jesus. The disciples tried to rebuke him. They were, after all, on their way to Jerusalem where Christ would be welcomed as King. But as this large procession of people moved toward Jerusalem, it says that Jesus "stopped." He engaged Bartimaeus in conversation, learned his need, and then ministered to him. Stopping, slowing down, turning off the road—all are acts that reflect the strength of Jesus' identification with disabled people.

If Jesus ...

IF JESUS IDENTIFIED SO deeply with us, and if he identified so deeply with people with disabilities, it can be our privilege to enter into a wonderful imitation of our Savior. We need not be intimate friends to identify. We need not be professional health-care workers to meet needs. We need not be theologians to value the essential worth of a disabled person. Submission to and imitation of Christ's way is all we need.

Part Two

Breaking Down Barriers

FOUR

Now You Know

Tracy, the mom on a mission in chapter 1, was so close to enjoying a new relationship with a person she would have otherwise ignored or even avoided. What she needed to help her step outside her world was a sense of identification with Lana. She needed to increase her value for people with disabilities as well as gain accurate information about them. That Tracy valued people there is no doubt. But her care had never been focused on those with disabilities. Compassion had moved her, but not far enough in the right direction.

What we need is to sharpen our understanding of the world of disability so that we can move in the right direction with compassion. Knowledge and love, acting in concert, can produce wonderful fruit in this case. But not only do we need to sharpen our understanding of disability, we also need concrete ideas on how to implement our desire to be a friend to a person with a disability.

This chapter will help you understand the different types of disabilities and what many disabled people share in common. Chapters 5 and 6 explore how you can initiate and grow a positive and comfortable relationship with those who have disabilities.

The Basics

UNDERSTANDING PEOPLE WITH DISABILITIES doesn't have to be complicated. True, there are plenty of strange-sounding medical terms for some disabilities, but it won't take you too long to become comfortable with the world of disability. A grasp of a few basic principles and a short catalog of the different types of disabilities will be all you need in order to start.

First, let's learn a good definition of the term "disability." The Americans with Disabilities Act (ADA) defines disability as a "physical or mental impairment that substantially limits one or more of the major life activities of an individual." Major life activities of a person might include such things as walking, breathing, speaking, seeing, etc. Being limited in any one of these activities will, in turn, affect a person's ability to participate in social, recreational, and employment opportunities. According to the National Organization on Disability, there are 49 million people in the U.S. to which this definition applies.

An important distinction needs to be made in this definition. Notice that a person has an "impairment." This is different than when we talk about a handicap. A handicap is an encumbrance in society or the environment that makes success more difficult to achieve. For example, stairs or a steep hill is a handicap. Lack of an attendant to help get up in the morning is a handicap. Poor attitudes on the part of employers is a handicap. All of these are outside of the person with a disability. That is why we don't typically refer to a person as being handicapped but rather that they encounter handicapping conditions.

Disability can no doubt dramatically affect a person's life. But we need to be careful in what we assume to be affected by the disability. Too many people have made incorrect assumptions about disabled people that have impeded or strained relationships with this community. There are basically four truths you need to keep in mind that apply to most people with disabilities. Remembering these truths will make you an outstanding friend.

Having a disability doesn't mean you're sick

Once a man sat down next to me, patted my knee, and sighed, "Oh, it's no fun being sick, is it?"

I gave him a curious look. "Uh . . . I don't have a cold or anything."

"No, no, no." He shook his head. "It's that wheelchair. I'm sorry you're sick," he said insistently.

I felt my defenses rising but bit my lip before I spoke. "Please sir, I want you to know that being in a wheelchair doesn't automatically make me sick," I said with gentle persuasion.

"Is that so?"

I nodded and smiled. I could tell a new attitude was taking shape.

Countless opportunities like that have given me the chance to set the record straight in people's minds. So please be mindful to treat a disabled person as a healthy individual. Just because the person has a functional limitation does not mean he is sick or diseased. Cerebral palsy is not a disease—it is any of several disorders of the nervous system. A broken neck or back is not an illness—it is an injury to the spinal cord. Polio is not a sickness—it is a handicapping condition that results from a virus. True, some disabilities are accompanied by health problems, but for the most part, disabilities are simply conditions or impairments.

Having a disability doesn't mean you have *all* the disabilities

Too many physically disabled people have been assumed to be unintelligent as well. Once in a while I go shopping with my friend Judy Butler. Store clerks sometimes ignore me and speak directly to Judy about my needs. "And what size does she wear? What color does she like?" The clerk acts as if I am unable to understand or answer such questions.

"I don't know, why don't you ask her" is Judy's patient response. And I'm not the only one to whom this has happened. Time and time again people without disabilities assume that a disability to one part of the person's body will somehow affect everything else.

This happens to people with mental disabilities just as easily. People often assume that they are hard of hearing and will talk to them in a loud voice. Unfortunately, I have met a few mentally disabled people who thought talking in a loud voice was natural to conversations because people always talked to them that way. They became loud talkers themselves.

Having a disability doesn't mean you don't have faith

On too many occasions people have challenged me to have faith in order to be healed. "All you need is faith, Joni, and God will heal you," I'm told. I appreciate their concern for me, and believe me, I'd be the first to dance for joy if I got out of this chair. They make a critical mistake when they assume my condition is dependent upon my faith and not on God's sovereignty.

Our bodies—our earthen vessels—are not direct reflections of the inner spirit. To be broken on the outside can, in fact, lead to greater faith. That is precisely what Paul experienced when he asked for a removal of the "thorn in the flesh." Was God's answer to Paul—a promise that his grace was sufficient—a rebuke of Paul's lack of faith? No. Paul, of all the New Testament characters, seems to have expressed the greatest of faith. His faith, as well as the faith of countless others who experienced suffering, was refined and made more splendid through his disability.

Having a disability doesn't mean you get a free ticket to heaven

People with disabilities, like all people who are morally and spiritually accountable, will stand before God the Judge and answer for the choices they have made in life. Did they respond to Christ's call and sacrifice? Or did they reject his grace? God will not say on that day, "You poor dear. You've suffered so much on earth. Seventy years in a wheelchair is quite a long time. Here, you can come into heaven on the basis that it wasn't your fault and I owe you one."

No! The sad thing about the whole matter is that unregenerate disabled people will not only have endured hardships on earth but they will also suffer in hell forever. That's a frightening reminder as to why it's so important to share the gospel among this forgotten field. Friendship for the purpose of evangelism couldn't be any more needed than with those in the disability community.

The preceding principles are foundational for your understanding of people with disabilities. If I were to summarize these principles into one theme, it would be this: think about and treat a person with a disability as if he or she were no different than you. That is hard to picture perhaps, given what I shared so far and what I am about to share about specific types of disabilities. But remember that the essence of a person—their capacity to think, feel, and choose—are affected but not eliminated by the disability. A disabled person is a whole person.

Physical Disabilities

WHEN IT COMES TO asking and answering questions about handicapping conditions, nobody does it better than kids. No topic is sacred!

Take my own paralysis. Come to think of it, even the word "paralysis" raises questions of its own. For children—or adults, for that matter—the word sounds frightening, yet very mysterious. A child's first question (yet not voiced until the third or fourth!) is how I manage in the bathroom. Others will notice my leg spasms and wonder how I can move—since I can't move!

A few kids think that being paralyzed is the same as being stiff or rigid. One boy asked if my body remained in the same sitting position when I was in bed. Of course, they always scratch their heads when they learn I can drive a van sixty-five miles an hour on the freeways!

Spinal cord injury

I had many of the same questions when I was admitted to the rehab hospital after my diving accident. There were people of every age on my wing. All of us were there because of spinal cord injuries. Some were straining to push their wheelchairs while others whizzed by in zippy power models. Still others were in bed with paralysis too limiting to even sit up. A few shuffled down the halls with walker aids. And there were those whose paralysis was much like mine—severe, but at least I was able to sit up.

It seemed strange at first. All of us were classed as having spinal cord injuries, and yet we were so different. That prompted me to ask my doctor a lot of questions. His explanation cleared my thinking and will help you too.

He told me the spinal cord is a bundle of nerve fibers and cells that connects the brain with muscles, skin, and internal organs. An injury, permanent or temporary, results when one of the vertebrae in the spinal column breaks and either bruises or cuts the cord.

The spinal cord can be injured at any point along its approximate twenty-five inches. Depending on the location of the damage, each injury has its own unique characteristics. Occasionally, the cord will be severed completely. Most often it will be badly bruised. Depending on which combination of "wires" remain intact, a wide range of functioning abilities result.

A total severance of the spinal cord means a person cannot feel or generate movement below the level of injury. Also, the higher the injury point, the greater loss of function. That's why some folks are up and about in walkers and others are hooked up to respirators simply to breathe. Functioning with a broken neck is quite different than functioning with a broken back.

For instance, a paraplegic has usually sustained an injury in the lower part of the spinal column, perhaps at the chest or lower back level. And the prefix "para" means half of the body is involved.

Quadriplegia, on the other hand, involves all four limbs of the body. A lesion (injury) in the spinal cord at the upper portion of the spine will usually result in paralysis of both arms and legs.

Although a great deal of research is going on right now to find a cure for spinal cord injury, the paralysis is usually permanent. The cord is unable to regenerate or repair itself. Unless a cure is developed (and unless the Lord intervenes with a divine healing!), people with SCI (a nifty abbreviation) can expect to deal with functional limitations.

There are nearly 250,000 persons in the United States who now are paralyzed as the result of a spinal cord injury. And every year 8,000 more are added. The number keeps going up because people in this country have very active, mobile lifestyles.

Muscular dystrophy

If you have ever seen a Jerry Lewis muscular dystrophy telethon, then you have a good idea of what MD is all about. Pictures of little children in leg braces may tug at your heart strings.

But what are the facts? Muscular dystrophy hits kids. It is a disease. One third of the 200,000 people in the United States who have this disease are between the ages of three and thirteen.

For the families of these young people, the reminder of muscular dystrophy is more than a special television feature on a holiday weekend. It is the day-in, day-out presence of a degenerative disease. While muscles have a normal appearance, they gradually weaken and the rate of progression is often rapid with no remission.

MD itself is not fatal. However, eventually all the voluntary muscles are affected. When they are too wasted to perform their functions in circulation and respiration, death results.

You can imagine the emotional and physical trauma that friends and families experience as they watch their loved one weaken. Your support is crucial. They need shoulders to cry on and hands to help. They need time away for refreshment and reminders that they are loved.

During the progress of this disease, the person will become disabled, requiring crutches, and then a wheelchair. Eventually they will be confined to bed. With this additional care, you may find yourself ministering more to the family than the young person who has MD. Remember, ministry may entail simple tasks like mowing the lawn, praying, bringing in meals, cleaning the house, reminding them of God's care, reading a book to the child, taking a brother or sister out for an ice cream cone—the possibilities of ways to help are unlimited.

Multiple sclerosis

Perhaps the most fickle disease that results in physical handicaps is multiple sclerosis. A quarter to a half million people in the United States alone have this neurological disease of the brain and spinal cord.

In multiple sclerosis, a substance called myelin, which insulates the nerve fibers, hardens and is replaced by scar tissue.

When the brain attempts to send messages to various parts of the body, the scar tissue distorts or blocks the impulses that control such functions as walking, talking, and vision.

Most frequently, multiple sclerosis strikes adults of either sex between the ages of twenty and forty. The disease may begin with a single relatively minor symptom such as blurred vision in one eye or weakness of a single limb. The symptom can disappear and no new warning signs show up for weeks, months, or even years. However, multiple sclerosis may begin as an acute, incapacitating illness that progresses rapidly downhill.

That is why it is so difficult to deal with MS. It's capricious. For a period of time a person with multiple sclerosis may not be able to write or tie her shoes or even feed herself. Then in a matter of weeks or months she may regain the ability to do those things.

You can imagine how having this disease is like riding an emotional roller coaster. The uncertainty is probably the hardest part. An ex-athlete may not know whether he will be able to walk without a cane next month. The young mother must decide if she should hire extra help for the children. An executive in his forties wonders if he should order a specially equipped van as the transfers into his sedan become more difficult. The emotional drain of dealing with multiple sclerosis only makes these decisions more difficult. According to my friend Bonnie who has multiple sclerosis, "Fatigue is the second hardest factor MSers encounter. We need our friends to be flexible and to understand when we have a last-minute necessity to cancel so that we won't be afraid of being excluded next time."

Traumatic Brain Injury (TBI)

Before I leave physical disabilities I should talk about one that is a "first cousin" to spinal cord injury. Although its symptoms are many and varied, it is known under the general category of head injury. Similar to SCI, it usually affects young, vigorous people who are injured in a sports accident or automobile mishap.

Its symptoms may include blindness, paralysis, loss of memory and impairment of mental function. Every year there are more than 140,000 people in the United States who die as a result of head injuries. Most of these deaths are the direct result of auto, motorcycle, or diving accidents. It would be an even higher number if not for modern medical techniques that save the lives of almost half that number. Often, however, those 50,000–70,000 are left permanently disabled. Modern miracles of medicine have saved them, but we are lagging far behind in helping them.

It is no wonder that head injuries, and the resulting permanent impairments, are often called the "Silent Epidemic." Oftentimes, someone who has been through this trauma will remain in a coma for several months before even regaining consciousness. It is common that people with head injuries may not have the concentration or memory they once had and may not be able to control their emotions. Awareness of this epidemic will help us to more sensitively reach out to this misunderstood group of disabled persons.

Cerebral palsy

This is a condition due to either damage or faulty development of the motor controls of the brain. The injury occurs either before or during birth. Sometimes the damage happens early in a youngster's life. CP is not degenerative. It may be mild spasticity and speech impairment, or it may be so severe that the individual needs to be strapped tightly into his wheelchair.

Why is so much social stigma attached to cerebral palsy? Perhaps fear and ignorance play a large role. As I have shared before, people will wrongly assume that an individual is mentally retarded if he sits in a wheelchair, is spastic, or cannot speak. Don't chalk up people with CP as mentally handicapped simply because they may shuffle their feet when they walk or drool when they eat.

True, some people with cerebral palsy may be retarded due to the brain injury. But don't assume so. Susie, my friend with CP, has a master's degree from a nearby seminary. John, another friend who communicates with a word board, is a published poet.

Communicate with someone who has cerebral palsy, and you will quickly see beyond the uncontrolled actions into the heart of one made in the image of God.

Those disabilities requiring adaptive equipment

Many physically handicapped people must use wheelchairs. Others use walkers, canes, or crutches. This adaptive equipment, as it's called, does not restrict physically disabled people. In fact, for me, a wheelchair liberates me to move about more freely. I wouldn't say I am confined to a wheelchair. My chair is not a lifelong sentence to some sort of mobile prison but a handy way of getting from one place to another. And with my power chair, I can get there by myself!

Occasionally I encounter a few architectural barriers when I'm scooting around. If it's a matter of a few steps, friends can lift my wheelchair. But not so with a flight of stairs. There have been many times when several men have wanted to carry me up a whole flight, but I've politely declined. Once I fell down a whole flight of stairs. And that did it for the old "love lifted me" routine.

So don't be offended if the person in a wheelchair rejects your offers to take the place of an elevator. Respect his wishes. Understand that his wheelchair is a heavy item, even without the added body weight. Your disabled friend may be genuinely concerned about hurting your back. In fact, I still struggle with guilt feelings when I think of a good friend of mine who still has back problems from lifting me nearly five years ago.

Other physically handicapping conditions

It would take volumes of medical textbooks to discuss every physically handicapping condition. I have merely touched on a few. More could be said about environmental illness, Alzheimer's, Fredrick's Ataxia, spina bifida, post-polio syndrome, and many others. Be informed. Brush up on the facts surrounding the disability of your friend. If you'd like to learn more, visit your local library.

Mental Disabilities

A MOTHER STORMED UP to one of the elders in our church, tugging her young son alongside. By the look on her face, you could tell she was about to explode. Pointing her finger at the elder, she stated her complaint: "I will not have my son participating in the same classroom with those idiots. For all I know, one of them will attack my son. Those mentally retarded children are totally unpredictable and dangerous. I'm taking my son elsewhere."

With that, she turned on her heels and led her son away.

This scenario is not all that uncommon. It is repeated in churches everywhere. People fear the mentally retarded. There are many misconceptions and distortions, and unfortunately, the young people who are retarded are the ones who suffer most.

The irate mother in church was perhaps confusing mental retardation with mental illness. The truth is, retardation is not an illness. The two are quite separate. Let me explain.

Mental illness is just that—an illness. It is sometimes caused by chemical imbalances. Often it results from deep-seated psychological problems. As an illness, it can be treated with medication, surgery, or counseling. Mental illness doesn't necessarily interfere with intellectual abilities. It might appear that way because it can be expressed in the form of irrational behavior or, on rare occasion, violence. Friends of those with mental illness are quick to point out that violence is not the norm. Unfortunately, society has believed the prevailing notion that mentally ill people need to be locked up precisely because of their potential for violence.

Mental retardation occurs at or near birth and is characterized by impaired intellectual development. Mental retardation is a term in the process of transition, even as I write this. Our friends at Special Olympics use the term "mentally challenged." Those in the political advocacy field find the term "mentally retarded" to be insulting. They use the term "intellectually disabled." Professionals often use the term "developmentally disabled." For the sake of simplicity, meanwhile, I will concur with my friends at the American Association for Mental Retardation (AAMR) and use the term "mentally retarded."

Mental retardation cannot be cured but can be treated through educational techniques, medication, or therapy. It is usually a lifelong condition. With understanding and patience, people who are mentally retarded are as giving, loving, and generous as the best of us.

Society has taken some real steps forward in helping people who are mentally retarded. Personally, I believe there are more services, agencies, family counseling opportunities, and other helps for the mentally retarded than most people are aware of. But, oh, the bureaucracy and red tape that exists! You or your church can serve as an advocate for someone who is mentally retarded, helping him locate the available resources.

Let me tell you about Rodney. Like a lot of the young fellows in our church, Rodney has really gotten involved. An active participant in church, he is often seen passing out bulletins at the front door before the Sunday morning service. Often Rodney will be running an errand to help his friend, a busy elder. He smiles a lot, lifting the spirits of those who come in contact with him.

But there is more to Rodney than just a helpful spirit. He is mentally retarded. He struggles with the ups and downs of being a teenager with a severe disability. He has known abuses and barriers as he has watched people keep a polite distance. Other kids go out on dates or drive cars. He has sat in the stands, watching his friends lead cheers and play football. He has played the role of a wallflower, observing his classmates at high school dances.

Yet Christ has given Rodney a deep sense of peace. He knows he is different. He understands he will never be quite like his friends in the college and career department. Still he knows that God loves him. That is because there are folks at church who express God's unconditional love every time they chat with Rodney or smile in return when he hands them a church bulletin.

What about people like Rodney? Do we want them relegated to a back room so we won't have to give any explanation for their behavior? Do we want their Sunday school class in the farthest corner of the church building—perhaps even with its own entrance—so they won't "offend" any visitors? We must remember they are as much a part of the family of God as the eldest and wisest of us. They leave us an example. For of such really is the kingdom of heaven.

Learning Disabilities

A LEARNING DISABILITY IS a disorder in things like speech, language, reading, or writing. The person with a learning disability processes such information differently and has a hard time learning. Dyslexia, for example, causes a person to perceive letters or numbers in a different order than a typical person would see them. Letter order might be reversed or even the letters themselves may looked reversed, as if in a mirror. It is an invisible disability that most of us don't realize exists, but it can create a lot of heartache for the individual.

The person with a learning disability can be an extremely intelligent person with many gifts. Unfortunately, our system of language, math, and communication may be inaccessible to him or her. Even though people with learning disabilities can become highly successful and productive members of society, there is always a level of frustration that will accompany them.

Visual Impairments

REMEMBER WHEN YOU PLAYED hide and seek? You would turn out the lights and make yourself as small as possible behind a piece of furniture. Every once in a while you would hear a snicker as the person who was "it" came near. When it was your turn to be "it," suddenly you couldn't remember the exact placement of the furniture. Bruises appeared on your shins the next day to show for it!

It wouldn't be a bad idea to play that game once in a while even as adults. It might increase our sensitivity to those who have visual impairments, making us more aware of their particular needs. It is easy to take our eyesight for granted.

That fact is becoming a reality to me. I have been painting a lot lately at my easel. The studio is a mess. Tracing paper is all over the floor, I get watercolor stains on my clothes, and I can never find my good erasers. But despite all that, I love the time I spend at my easel.

It is that love that is getting me into trouble. You see, I get carried away and paint for hours. Before you know it, my neck gets a cramp and I notice my jaw aches from clamping so hard on the brush.

But what I really notice is my eyes. They never used to bother me. But this year it has begun to dawn on me that my eyes are not what they used to be. After even one hour at my easel, I have noticed that objects at a distance are getting blurry.

I have new prescription glasses. And in months to come I will have to be more careful to rest my eyes every twenty minutes or so. Good clear eyesight is precious and worth every precautionary measure. In the United States, 2.4 million people have severe visual impairments. That statistic reminds us to be thankful for the gift of sight.

The senses of smell, touch, or hearing do not improve when a person becomes blind. It is just that the blind person relies on these senses more. Therefore, they may receive more information through those senses than most people. They can, as they put it, "feel" someone next to them. Blind individuals can "hear" a wall in front of them. They can sometimes "smell" someone coming down the street!

Let's crack some stereotypes about people who are blind. May I tell you about my friend, Amy? She is a young, pretty girl who graduated from college. She is also totally blind. Amy makes her way with a cane, preferring not to use a seeing eye dog. (She explains that, for her, it is too much bother to care for, feed, and exercise a dog.)

Amy loves bright and pretty colors in her clothes. She dresses with flair. She organizes her closets so that she doesn't confuse plaids with polka dots, bright pinks with muted greens. Many of the clothes she wears she has sewn herself.

This active, outgoing friend of mine loves God's Word. She reads the Bible in braille and when she wants to highlight a certain verse, she will staple it. How's that for creativity?

Amy's story reminds me of an illustration my pastor shared at church. It had to do with a young blind girl who had met the Lord and fell in love with his Word. Much like Amy, she read braille. In fact, this girl read so much that she developed calluses on her fingertips.

When she could no longer "read" because of the calluses, she began peeling them back to expose more sensitive tissue under the skin. Unfortunately, the raw and sore skin became permanently damaged and she could no longer read the braille pages of her Bible.

Sadly, she had to part with her braille Bible. So lifting the bulky manuscript to her lips, to kiss it good-bye, she discovered that she could feel. Her lips picked up the various braille indentations. She had found a new way to keep in touch with God's Word.

When I hear stories like this or think of my friend Amy, it seems my disability isn't that big a deal. I can read God's Word. Although my fingers can't turn pages, I'm able to nudge a page by mouthstick. Whether with lips or a mouthstick, it can be done!

Hearing Impairments

EVER WONDER WHICH DISABILITY, blindness or deafness, would be the most difficult to deal with?

Helen Keller, both deaf and blind, answered that question. "Blindness separates you from things. But deafness separates you from people."

That quote took on new meaning for me a few years ago. My friends who are hearing impaired had told me that one of the greatest difficulties the deaf deal with is paranoia. Picture it. A deaf person is with a group of people with whom he can't communicate. He sees them gesture, he watches them laugh, he looks at their lips move. He may think he's missing out on the fun, or he may think he's the object of a joke.

I can almost identify! Ken and I were in Switzerland to speak at a few meetings. Several German-speaking Swiss people escorted us as we journeyed from town to town. They were delightful folks and their English was good, but most of the time they enjoyed conversing together in their native tongue. I tried to pick up meaning from their sentences but it was impossible. At the dinner table I watched them chatter, gesture, and giggle. Occasionally they would look in our direction and warmly smile.

No doubt, these Swiss friends were having a grand conversation about positive things ... the results of the meetings, people who had accepted Christ, the disabled who attended the crusade.

But, frankly, I kept fighting off the same paranoia that deaf people so often feel. I watched them, trying hard to understand, yet to no avail. Ken and I longed to be involved in their conversation. At times, I thought they were talking about us.

Because I experienced a real communication barrier myself, I can better appreciate what deaf people go through.

Since then, I have picked up pointers that will be useful as you reach out to somebody who is hearing impaired or deaf.

First, definitions can be confusing. A person who is profoundly deaf is one for whom the sense of hearing is nonfunctional for ordinary purposes of life, particularly for understanding speech. On the other hand, someone who is hard of hearing may have a defective sense of hearing but can still hear and understand speech, especially with the help of a hearing aid and lipreading.

It is unwise to use phrases like "deaf mute" or "deaf and dumb." (Better to say, "My friend is deaf and doesn't speak.") It is like using the words "cripple" or "invalid." Those words carry negative connotations. Instead, use appropriate words like "deaf," "hard of hearing," or "hearing impaired."

People who are deaf are not mentally retarded. They have normal intellectual capabilities. However, they may lag behind academically because of the language barrier. You can imagine trying to learn a foreign language from somebody who is standing on the other side of a soundproof glass—especially if the two of you have no language in common! Difficult? That's often what it's like for a deaf child to learn English.

How Is Your Comfort Level?

CAN YOU SEE HOW getting your information straight can improve your comfort level? And if you don't know the facts, just ask.

I have thrown a lot of facts at you in this chapter. Yet if you still are uncomfortable with the idea of reaching out to a person whose disability you can't even pronounce, remember that you don't need to know everything about a person or their circumstances in order to be a friend. Discovery is one of the wonderful benefits of friendship. What you don't know before entering the relationship, you will discover as you go along.

FIVE

What to Say, How to Listen

L OVE.
What do you think of when you see that word? Do you picture a man and a wife at the altar saying their vows? How about a father and son walking hand in hand with a fishing pole? An elderly woman gently stroking her husband's hand as he lays in the hospital? A brother carrying his sister's books to school?

The pictures we associate with that word vary from person to person. But common to all of them is the value each one holds for the other. To love is to treasure another person. When we love, we calculate the worth of that person and find that we cannot begin to name the price. Our love invests a person with incalculable worth.

To befriend a person with a disability by identifying with them is to love them. By being a friend we say to them that they are of worth to us. We esteem them highly enough to know about their lives and to consider their needs important. We find creative ways to share that love so that the person is convinced of our heart's desire.

Funny thing, though, about such love. No matter how much we love someone, we often fail in our expressions of love. This is the case in any kind of love, not just for those with a disability.

For example, have you ever seen a husband and wife at odds with each other, and yet you knew they loved each other? The man floods her with flowers and chocolates, but she complains he never talks to her. She spends hours telling him what a wonderful provider he is, while he complains that the house is a mess. "If he loved me ... If she loved me ..." is heard often in such cases.

Both people really do love each other. But somehow the message doesn't get through. You might find the same as you share your friendship with a person with a disability. Your attempts at befriending someone may fall on hearing-impaired ears!

Gary Chapman would say that situations like this can stem from a love language problem. Gary wrote an interesting book about love called *The Five Languages of Love*. In it, he describes how love is expressed in different ways. Each of us naturally chooses a way to express love in a way that is most comfortable to us. Likewise, we tend to like to be loved in the way that we would express love. There are five ways of expressing love—words of affirmation, quality time, acts of service, physical touching, and receiving gifts.

Your relationship with a person with a disability can grow through the use of one or more of these love languages. The next two chapters provide ideas for each type of language. Remember, your use of these languages need not be reserved for a person with a disability with whom you have developed a deep friendship. We can show love to even a stranger and be a friend to them in just a passing gesture.

Say It with Words

"A WORD FITLY SPOKEN is like apples of gold in a setting of silver," says Proverbs 25:11 (RSV).

But how do I share my words with someone with a disability? you wonder. *I don't even know how to greet people with disabilities, let alone get into a conversation!*

Here is the good news about starting conversations. Approach it the same way you would any other first-time conversation. You may be waiting in the grocery line together, attending the same party, sitting next to each other at a PTA meeting, sitting near each other in Sunday school. Discuss the sorts of things you would normally. Smile, ask her name, where she is from, and so on. Converse naturally. Don't feel you must ask about the disability—especially if you sense she is uncomfortable with her handicap or unwilling to discuss it.

On the other hand, it may be wise not to ignore the person's disability either. In some cases, such as with those who are deaf or nonverbal, it is impossible to avoid—if you don't acknowledge the disability, how will you communicate?

If it seems natural to open up the topic of disabilities, it can be appropriate to ask sensitive questions. Most disabled people don't mind helping you to understand. You might say something like:

"Pardon me, may I ask you a personal question? How did you become paralyzed?"

"Excuse me, but I'm interested in your disability. Could you tell me how you came to be in a wheelchair?"

Of course, the key word is *appropriate*. There may be times and places when such questions come up in the middle of a conversation. Use common sense. Be sensitive. Never ask questions out of morbid curiosity; ask because you want to communicate care and interest.

Eye-to-Eye Conversation

I'VE OCCASIONALLY NOTICED THAT people's eyes start drifting downward when they are talking to me. They are mouthing words, but I can tell their attention is on my legs or my hands resting on my lap. I can almost tell what they are thinking. How does she keep her legs in shape? I wonder if her shoes show wear on the soles? Why do her fingers curl so?

All of us, able-bodied and disabled, enjoy eye-to-eye conversations. It is especially important to remember this when meeting a disabled person—more so when the muscles in his face are tightly drawn in contortion. If the person has lost control of certain facial muscles, he may have difficulty swallowing and may drool. If you look at that person in the eyes, you soon forget their differences. Do you remember the saying, "The eyes are the window of the soul"? Looking at a person in this way, you appreciate their heart and forget their appearance.

God does the same with us. He reminded Samuel, "The Lord does not look at the things man looks at. Man looks on the outward appearance, but the Lord looks at the heart."

The conversation widens if the disabled person has a companion. Don't forget the person who is standing behind the wheelchair. Often he or she remains in the shadow of his or her disabled friend. On the other hand, don't carry on a monologue with the companion. View these people as separate individuals. Don't always assume that they are a "pair" who enjoy the same interests or have the same opinions.

Treat a person age-appropriately, using the same tone of voice as you would if they were able-bodied. Please be careful not to "talk down" to those of us with physical disabilities. The following is virtually a transcript of an actual conversation.

"Oh, dearie, you look so sweet today," the lady in the large-flowered print dress said as she stooped and patted my cheek.

"Yes ... well, thank you," I stammered.

"You always look so pretty. And your nails!" she pressed her hand to her cheek.

"My nails?" I looked to see what she thought was so unusual.

"Well I must be going," she stroked my hair. "Ta."

I wonder if that woman would have conversed that way if I were standing up. Somehow I can't imagine her stroking and patting me, a forty-seven-year-old woman, if I were on my feet. Be mindful not to treat disabled people like children. Deal with a disabled person on an age-appropriate level.

And remember our necks! When people approach me who are very tall, sometimes I get a crick in my neck after speaking with them for a while. For better visibility, stand a few feet away. That puts us more on the same level. Also, you will want to stand directly in front of a person who cannot turn his or her head to the side due to inflexible neck muscles.

If you are going to have a long conversation, the very best idea is to pull up a chair and sit eye level with someone in a wheelchair. It makes it a lot easier to carry on a conversation face-to-face.

These suggestions may seem obvious, but you would be surprised how many people scratch their heads, wondering what to do in the same situations.

Getting into a Conversation … with Someone Who Can't Speak!

ONE MORNING AFTER CHURCH a young woman with cerebral palsy approached me in her wheelchair. Her speech was difficult to understand, and she kept repeating a certain sentence over and over. Even though I patiently asked her to slowly repeat each word, I still could not understand. I couldn't tell if she was in terrible trouble or was simply trying to communicate an exciting experience. Finally, I got the message. She wanted me to help her find someone who could assist her into the restroom. A simple request. And I felt so helpless, so inadequate, because I took so long to understand her. But I sure did rush to get her help!

That incident helped underscore the importance of learning to communicate with someone with labored speech, somebody who has cerebral palsy or has suffered a stroke.

Sure, it's uncomfortable to go up and greet someone only to discover they cannot talk. Don't panic. Your friend who cannot speak has encountered nervous people like you a hundred times before. Consider it a challenge the two of you will work out together. Your friend would probably be encouraged too if you admitted, "You know, I've never done this before. That is, talk to someone whose words I can't understand. But I'd sure like to try."

The first step? Ask if they have a word board. A word board is a communication device, commonly used by nonverbal people. It may have letters of the alphabet that a person can point to to construct a sentence. Other word boards list commonly asked questions such as, "May I have a drink of water?" or "Would you find my attendant?" Another communication device is a small computer that prints a message as the person pushes certain keys.

If he doesn't have a word board, go to the next step. Find out what his sign or signal is for *yes* or *no*. Begin by asking, "What's your signal for *yes*?"

In response, he may look up at the ceiling ... shake his foot ... wink once ... or any number of other signals. When you spot the sign, you might say something like, "Is winking once your sign for *yes*?" And they will wink once. Easy.

Once you both understand the common language, you can carry on a regular conversation by playing twenty questions. Find out his name, find out his interests. I have often said, "My name is Joni. I'd love to know what your name is. Does it start with an A, B, C, D ... ?" I continued until I was able to spell the person's name. (I hoped it wasn't Zelda!)

There may be a time when a nonverbal person approaches you with a special need. Just ask some basic questions. It would assure them if you said, "I cannot understand you. I'm going to try to figure out what you're saying. First of all, are you in any kind of pain?"

They might say or sign *no*.

You can continue, "Do you need something?"

And again their response is *no*.

"Is there anything wrong with your wheelchair?"

They might shake their head *yes*.

"Would you like me to take the brakes off?" Take a closer look at his wheelchair. "Is your cushion uncomfortable?" Take it from there, asking basic questions.

Like my story of the girl who needed help to the restroom, it may not be easy to understand what your new friend is trying to tell you. But she will understand that you cared enough to stop, to be real with her, to be quiet, and to listen.

Conversations with Hearing Impaired People

DON'T BE AFRAID TO talk directly to your deaf friend. Even if you need an interpreter to communicate, look at the deaf person as you talk. Doing this lets her know that you want to get to know her, not necessarily the interpreter whose hands you must "borrow." (Don't even ask the interpreter, "Would you ask him his name?" . . . the deaf person may surprise you and read your lips!)

Often there won't be an interpreter around to help. For such times, it is good to learn some sign language. Deaf people will appreciate your effort. Also, keep a notepad and pencil handy to write messages. Planning ahead shows your desire to communicate.

Sometimes deaf people have the ability to use their voices. Most deaf individuals prefer not to do so, though, because of the poor quality of their speech. But if somebody is trying to communicate and you don't understand what he is saying, never pretend that you do. Instead, ask the person to repeat what he said or to write it down on paper. Remember, he is probably used to repeating. Also, encourage him to ask you to repeat if he doesn't catch what you are saying.

Some more hints:

If you are aware that the hard-of-hearing person has a better ear, stand or sit on that side. They will be able to hear much better, too, if you cut down on the background noise.

Speak clearly, naturally, and at a moderate pace. It won't help to yell or exaggerate—you may be harder to understand! Both of these often result in distortion of speech.

Don't cover your face with your hands or objects. Many deaf people rely totally or partially on lip reading. So remember not to talk too fast.

Not long ago I was invited to speak at a church made up entirely of deaf and hearing-impaired people. As I talked from the platform, I noticed the pastor stood very close to me as he signed. In fact, his hands were right near my face. I learned later that he wanted to keep his hands near me so the deaf individuals in his congregation could read my facial expressions, and watch his interpretation at the same time.

I spied an elderly gentleman in the crowd who had his back to me. He was crouched over the hands of a young man who was facing me, his eyes intently fixed on my lips, glancing every once in a while at the pastor's interpretation. I noticed the older man hardly moved at all and seemed to crouch closer to his friend's hands when I was sharing an interesting point.

After I finished speaking, I learned that the man was not only deaf, but also blind. Since he could not see the pastor's interpretations or see my lips, he depended on the expert signing of the young man. His hands, aged and wrinkled, were cupped around the fingers, which gave him my message. Crouched close, he felt every single letter.

Curiously, the pastor mentioned to me that his deaf congregation considered the man to be the one who was really handicapped. He was hoping his congregation would be stimulated to reach out to meet the needs of people like the deaf-blind man.

Even disabled people need awareness!

What Words Can I Use?

THERE'S A LOT OF talk these days about politically correct language. Do we say Hispanic or Latino? Black or African-American? Oriental or Asian? The same debate is true for the world of disability. Just exactly what are we supposed to say or not say when describing people with disabilities? Frankly, I am bothered by those who take great offense at those who don't use just the right language. Rather, I think it's important to remember the effects of labels, no matter what word is being used. Even acceptable words like "disabled" or "handicapped" or "impaired" or "physically challenged" can become sticky labels when we refuse to see these people as persons first—individuals with hopes and dreams, opinions and interests. We need to view people with disabilities as persons, not conditions.

"She's a deafie" or "he's a retard" are labels that communicate more harm than good. Those statements say that the handicap is more obvious than the person. Instead, it would be better to say, "the girl who is deaf" or "the boy who is mentally retarded."

There are a few more careless words that are negative or just plain inaccurate. So that you can steer clear of such words, here are some no-no's from the dictionary of the disabled.

Avoid the word *afflicted.* Many disabled people feel that word makes them out to be victims. *Cripple* and *invalid* also have negative connotations.

Burden or *a drain* are more words to avoid. Many disabled people don't consider their impairment a burden. The disability simply presents a few added responsibilities.

Do be careful how you use the word *suffers*. "She suffers from blindness" or "he suffers from a spinal cord injury" just may not be true. If a person with a disability is independent and copes with life successfully, then that word does not apply any more than it would for an able-bodied person. To tell the truth, I suffer a lot more when I have the flu than when I cope with my everyday routines in a wheelchair.

Disabled people are not *handicaps* or *poor unfortunates*. What is unfortunate is that these words are often used to describe people who live happy and meaningful lives. A person who is handicapped is not necessarily a *victim*. Let's be mindful that his disability has been permitted by God for a very special reason.

My goal in giving you this list is to ask your aid in keeping disabled people from sounding pitiful or inferior. If we can avoid using these words in everyday language, then we will do a great service not only to the disabled community, but we go a long way toward correcting our own attitudes at the same time.

A Time to Love

YOU CAN BE A wonderful friend to a person with a disability simply by investing your time. We live in a "hurry up world." Many people with disabilities sense that when a nondisabled person visits them, especially in a nursing home or other type of residential facility, the nondisabled friend is on his or her way somewhere else or impatient to get home. People with disabilities have often grown accustomed to professionals who can't linger because there are other "clients" to visit. Your use of time can dispel the notion that nondisabled people have more important things to do.

How can you use time to communicate love?

Consider my friend Jackie. She came to me on a painful night and knew I needed help. She simply climbed into bed, lay next to me, and held my hand. It felt good to have someone that near. In the quiet darkness she sang hymns. I will never forget, "Man of Sorrows, what a Name. For the Son of God who came. Ruined sinners to reclaim. Hallelujah! What a Savior."

Those words sung quietly in the still night were a creative expression of comfort and care. Jackie empathized; she did not say, "I know what you're going through, Joni." She simply, quietly ministered. And you know what? Jackie didn't disappear after the novelty of the hospital stay wore off.

By the time three months in the hospital had passed, I noticed that only committed friends continued coming by. Visiting week in and week out called for not only commitment on their part but creativity as well. Creativity, before and after the fact, is an exceptional quality in any friend.

Jackie's words certainly ministered to me, but more than that, it was her presence that calmed me and showed that she was my friend. Go to any group home where people with disabilities live and I guarantee you will have friends for life if you simply sit in the activity room or on the porch and watch the world go by. That was one of Steve's favorite times at the Christian League for the Handicapped where he worked as director. After a busy day at the office, he would sit out under the verandah and watch the cars go by with some of the residents—Norm, Jon, Tom, and Birdie. Or he would hang out in the kitchen during break time and engage in some good-hearted kidding.

An investment of your time doesn't have to interrupt your schedule. You can include a person with a disability as you go about your day. Whether it's asking them to join you on your trip to the mall or working beside you in the garden, you are saying a lot to a person about how you value them. You are expressing a sense of desire for their inclusion in your private life.

Critical to investing time is the activity of listening. Good listeners make great friends. Listening may be as simple as letting the other person unload, but there are some specific things you should know.

When your friend wants to recount memories of life before the disability

Don't worry. They are not crying in their soup. Enjoy the memories with them. There is something comforting about sharing memories. Especially if you are disabled and have fond memories of days when you weren't always in a wheelchair. Even the apostle Paul wrote from prison to his friends and reassured them that his suffering was soothed by the joy of memories. He started out his letter to the Philippians, "I thank God every time I remember you."

Nice memories . . . I still like to talk about them. They have a way of bolstering our spirits and inspiring us through long stretches of difficulties.

I thank the Lord for friends who don't mind listening if I feel like recounting memories. I remember the feel of my wet feet walking on the warm concrete apron of a swimming pool. I remember the feel of wet leather reins in my hands when I would ride my horse. And on a hot day it was a relief to feel the chill of an ice-cold bottle of Coke in my grip. When I would jog with my friends, I recall the exhausting, yet exhilarating sensation of working muscles.

Snapping flowers off their stems. Scouring a sink with sponge and cleanser. Creaming my own hands. Having my ankles rubbed. Feeling my fingers on the ivory keys of a piano. Brushing a horse's coat. Drumming my fingers on a desk. These and so many other remembrances help me to not take for granted those things I still can feel and do. And their joy is multiplied if shared with a friend . . . a listening friend. What comfort!

When your friend feels like crying

Compassion and open-ended commitment begins with allowing others time to cry. There is a time to weep and mourn, as the Bible says. We cannot expect newly disabled people to dry their tears and listen to our well-rehearsed Bible passages about suffering, hoping they will change overnight. They need time. Friends who lack real compassion find it difficult to give others time to adjust or accept a disability. Impatiently, they look for immediate results of their prayers and efforts.

But who can be impatient with the tears of someone who has lost so much? Especially one with a disability? For example, when I cry, I can't wipe my eyes. I lean forward and let the tears drop onto my lap. But that makes my nose run. And I can't even reach for a Kleenex. You can imagine, I'm a real mess when I cry. The frustration of it all makes me want to cry all the more!

So if there are rules on how to be a compassionate friend to a disabled person, the first would be to sincerely carry their emotional baggage. Allow your friend the freedom to express himself. Let him cry. Better yet, cry with him. We are even told to do that in Romans 12:15: "Weep with those who weep" (RSV).

When your friend is angry

But your friend may not be the crying type. Perhaps his emotions are better vented through anger. It is natural for a newly disabled person to shake a fist at God. "You say God's allowed this? Humph. With friends like him, who needs enemies!" he may say.

Our reaction is to gasp in horror when we hear that kind of anger directed at God. But nothing your friend says is a surprise to God. He knows your friend's thoughts before they come out of his mouth. Review Psalm 139 as a reminder of how personally God knows each one of us. Phrases like " ... you have searched me and you know me ... you perceive my thoughts from afar ... you are familiar with all my ways.... Before a word is on my tongue you know it completely, O LORD."

Allow your friend freedom to express his anger. It may even be directed at you some of the time. Commit yourself to hear it—and forget it. God doesn't need a defense lawyer. This is not the time to set any records straight. Nor is it the time to make a mental note of all that is said out of distress so that it can be brought up later. Remember that wonderful chapter of love in action, 1 Corinthians 13? One of the attributes of love is that we don't keep a record of wrongs—not for ourselves or anyone else. Not even for God! The same idea is voiced in Proverbs 10:12: "Love covers over all wrongs."

I must, however, add an important and personal note. There was a certain point when several compassionate friends simply put their foot down and refused to put up with my anger or tears any further. They realized that was the loving thing to do. I am sure they had to be extra sensitive to the Spirit's leading and to my condition to do such a thing. But I'm glad their commitment was deep enough to risk my rejection.

When your friend is having doubts

Give the disabled person room for doubt. We all doubt at one time or another, and I wonder why we refuse to admit it (as though it were shameful). There certainly are examples of Christians who doubted in the Bible. The disciple Thomas said in so many words, "I don't believe it, but I sure would like to." The father of the boy with an evil spirit said, "I do believe; help me overcome my unbelief." Somehow I think Jesus read his heart and understood his quandary.

Can you understand how easy it would be to doubt God if you just learned you had a terminal illness? Can you empathize with someone who only recently discovered he had to have his leg amputated? Doubts are common among the disabled. Don't be caught off guard. Have faith on the behalf of your friend who lacks it. God can even give him faith to still doubt—and yet believe.

Look again at the story in Luke 10. It is significant that the Samaritan didn't show his love by taking the injured man straight to church. Instead he took him to an inn where real healing could begin. There were no platitudes, no dropping a coin in the coffer. No, the Good Samaritan not once trivialized the injured man's misfortune with prepackaged Bible verses or a pat on the head.

The injured man may have cried. He may have been angry. He could have even doubted God. The Good Samaritan, however, showed the compassionate, committed response. But what he did along the road was only the beginning.

Love with meaning

Being a friend involves communicating your love in ways that have meaning and in ways that impart who you are. Communicating through words and time can transform a life and create a wonderful path of growth, for both you and the person with a disability. And for those of you who like to *do* something about your love? Read on. Your chance to shine is coming!

SIX

More Than Words

SOME OF YOU HAVE been designed by God to enjoy the activities of love. You love to *do* things for people. You love to *give*. And your ministry of *touching*—gentle strokes and giant hugs are notorious. You are saying "It's about time we got down to the important stuff! Tell me what to do!"

So, for those of you wired this way, here is the "good stuff." That doesn't mean that those of you who loved chapter 5 can skip this chapter. No. Remember that love is not how you want to express it but how the person with a disability will receive it. So stick with us as we explore creative ways of loving through action.

How Can I Help?

THE FIRST STEP TO friendship through doing involves a very simple muscle found on your face—your smile! A smile is a great place to start. Who doesn't like to be on the receiving end of a sincere smile? Like that advertisement about the "friendly skies," it makes us want to pass on the kindness that has been shown to us. How does that old saying go? "Smile and the whole world smiles with you."

Wise King Solomon knew that. In Proverbs he wrote, "A happy heart makes the face cheerful" and "A cheerful look brings joy to the heart." If we are going to reach out to the disabled with God's joy, it has to be translated from our heart to the heart of the disabled friend. Here is the key—joy in our hearts is best demonstrated by our smiles, and that can bring joy to the hearts of others. Though not a profound concept, a smile is a good beginning for any of us who want to show Jesus' love.

Sure you may be shy. Smiling at strangers (whether in wheelchairs or not) doesn't come easily. But you have to start somewhere. And like anything we feel uncomfortable with, it takes practice. Ask God for courage, then greet those around you with a smile—able-bodied and disabled alike. Start with family and good friends. Sometimes they are the ones who see your cheerful smile the least. As your smile becomes a more natural part of your conversation, add it to your "thank you" to the paperboy or bank teller. With a little practice, a smile will come easily.

Don't forget though—treat the disabled as you would any other person. If you are comfortable with smiling and greeting people in church, then smile and greet the deaf girl at the end of the pew. And wouldn't it make her day to have you learn the sign for "hello" or "good to see you"?

Incidentally, some people are hesitant about smiling and greeting those with disabilities for fear that the friendliness will be misconstrued as pity. Don't worry—your rule of thumb should be to greet disabled people as you would anyone else. But one word of caution: disabled people have a way of seeing right through your motives. If you do foster pity, then prayerfully examine your own motives before reaching out to others. Pity—that condescending attitude that "feels sorry" for others—never helps anyone.

Offering a Hand

As you would for anyone, please do offer your assistance if you see a way to help. If you spot someone wheeling his chair toward a door, simply ask, "Do you need some help?" Offering assistance is a common courtesy. Wait for a reply, though, before going ahead. And if the person says, "No, thanks," that's okay. At least you have offered.

Remember though, each paralyzed person will answer differently. Some of my best friends who are quads have vastly different opinions on their disabilities and personal routines. Perhaps that's why you need to ask questions. There is a group of us who loved to be asked if we needed help getting into a department store. Until malls started installing automatic sliding doors, I would sometimes wait long minutes before a shopper came by to help.

How can you best help her? You will never know until you ask. Say, for instance, you are dining with a SCI person for the first time. The conversation may run something like this:

"Hamburgers look good, don't they?" Jennifer said as she leaned on her wheelchair armrests to get a good look at the menu.

"Are you planning to order one?" Melissa asked.

"No," her friend sighed, "I'm really not that hungry."

Melissa knew that was not the case. She prayed for the right words, not wanting to force her friend to do more than she could.

"Jennifer, you mentioned you were hungry just an hour or two ago. I don't want to force you, but if you're willing to order something, I'm willing to help."

"Well ... uh," Jennifer sighed, "my hands don't work well enough to grab a big-sized burger."

"Hey," Melissa said, "no problem, I'll be happy to give a hand. Just let me know what to do."

The girl in the wheelchair smiled demurely. "That's okay," she said in a polite whisper, glancing at the other patrons in the restaurant. "I really would rather not be fed. You know, it just looks ... well, funny. Besides, I'm not very neat," she concluded her argument.

Melissa reached over and touched the armrest of her friend's wheelchair. "I understand. But if you're really into hamburgers, I can easily cut the entire thing up for you, bun and all. You can handle it using your special spoon."

Jennifer seemed surprised at the suggestion. "You'd do that? Uh ... thanks. I guess I will order a double burger with extra onions after all," she laughed. There was a thoughtful pause. "You know, I was expecting you not to understand my feelings ... thought you'd give me a lecture about being fed in public. Thanks for being a friend, a real friend."

The girl in our story used a special spoon. You see, many disabled people are able to feed themselves. A burger may have to be cut up, a glass may have to be lifted, or a napkin may have to be unfolded and placed in a lap, but many manage very well with only occasional help.

But suppose our story went differently:

Camille wasn't sure how she and her disabled friend, Nadine, ended up in a restaurant. She was only planning to wheel Nadine to the mall. But here they were, and Camille nervously surveyed the table. What should she do first?

"Mind spreading my napkin on my lap?" Nadine suggested.

Of course, Camille thought to herself, silly me—why didn't I think of that?

"Mind if I look at the menu with you?" said Nadine.

Camille was losing what little appetite she had. All she could think of was how stupid she felt. She bravely asked the obvious question, "What do you plan to order?"

Nadine glanced over the page. "A hamburger with extras," she said smiling. "You don't mind feeding me, do you?" she said with a confidence which surprised Camille.

Camille hesitated. "Great, but ... uh, I've never fed any-body a hamburger." She could just see herself smashing too much of the hamburger into her friend's mouth, squirting ketchup everywhere, and scattering french fries on the floor. She took another deep breath and then said, "Mind if you're a guinea pig?"

"You'll do fine," Nadine said to put her friend at ease.

"Okay, but just let me know when you want a bite."

Her friend in the wheelchair leaned forward as if to share a secret. "We can shorten it—when you see me finish a bite, then just give me another!"

A conversation like this can happen anytime. As in the case of our two stories, sometimes the able-bodied helper confi-dently knows what to do; other times, the disabled person gives all the helpful directions. As was already shared, disabled people have different ways of dealing with different situations.

I want to reemphasize the importance of allowing your dis-abled friend to do as much as she can for herself. If she is learn-ing to feed herself, let her. Even if she spills and drops things, encourage her anyway. As her friend, you can gently nudge her toward greater independence.

Above all, keep a sense of humor! Things will go wrong, so learn not to take these circumstances too seriously. Flat tires on the wheelchair, the insensitivity of people, leaking leg bags, inaccessi-ble buildings, spilled food, spasms ... even one of these can set us into a tailspin on our best of days if we let it. So learn to laugh.

For example, let me tell you about one of "those" times. I had been asked to speak at a conference and had been intro-duced on stage. As I was making my way to the microphone, I realized I still had a big wad of bubble gum in my mouth.

I didn't dare keep chomping away on that gum and so I quickly lifted my arm to my mouth and stuck it on the leather of my hand splint.

I positioned myself in front of the microphone, forgot about the gum, smiled at the congregation, breathed a quick prayer, and started speaking.

Toward the middle of my message, I got excited about a favorite Bible verse. With exaggerated gestures, I emphasized each point.

After a few minutes I heard giggles ... then muffled laughter from the second row.

I looked at my lap and, to my horror, the wad of gum was stuck to everything—the arm of my wheelchair, my slacks, and my sweater. With all that gesturing I had woven an incredible web of bubble gum all over the front of me. Somehow the gum had even attached itself to the microphone stand. I was mortified!

There was no way I could continue. I laughed a bit disconcertedly with the crowd while a kind soul from the first row came and untangled me.

At that point, my message changed to something about the friends of Lazarus unraveling him from his web of graveclothes. Needless to say, it was pretty hard to get back to the serious message I had prepared.

We all have those days, so keep your sense of humor. Because you are more removed from the situation than your handicapped friend, you can have a real part in making those "mountains into molehills." Perhaps on those days you can put Galatians 6:9 to the test: "Let us not become weary in doing good, for at the proper time we will reap a harvest if we do not give up."

If it means cleaning up extra messes, taking more time to fix a flat on a wheelchair, interrupting your day to do unexpected errands—whatever it takes—you can help lighten the day for your friend. You may even laugh about it tomorrow.

If you don't want to be weary in doing good today, then you need to have a sense of humor. No one likes to feel like they're a burden. And by keeping a sense of humor while you help your disabled friend, you'll elevate your service to a joy. And that's a long way from making your friend feel like a millstone around your neck.

Paraplegics in wheelchairs are able to grocery shop independently but may need help with items from the top shelves or to reach the scales to weigh their fruits and vegetables. While more and more businesses are including services to help people with disabilities, it's still fun for you to offer this kind of assistance.

Consider these activities from the Christian League for the Handicapped:

Offer transportation to a handicapped person on a regular basis.

Learn some basic sign language to communicate your friendship to a person who is deaf.

Don't park you car in spaces designated for the disabled.

Hold the door open for a person in a wheelchair or on crutches in a shopping center, at church or wherever. It's a common courtesy, but often overlooked.

Offer to provide transportation to the store, to church, to the doctor's office, or to a social gathering. Transportation for those who are mobility impaired is a real problem, even in big cities.

There are many people with disabilities who are extremely capable of getting around town. But minor emergencies can happen. You might be asked to pick up something that has been dropped, push a wheelchair that has lost its power, dial a phone for someone who is deaf—the possibilities are unlimited. Your willingness and availability is a demonstration of Christ's love to those in need.

You may come across someone who is blind standing by an elevator. It's okay to ask if you may press the floor button for them, especially if the buttons are not marked in braille. It's also thoughtful to hold the elevator door open for someone less ambulatory as they make their way out onto the floor.

The National Federation of the Blind has put out some courtesy rules to remember when meeting someone who is blind:

First, as with anyone who has a disability, please remember that blind folks are ordinary people. You don't need to raise your voice or address them as though they were children. Rather, talk to them as you would anyone else. Be certain to direct the questions to the person who is blind, rather than to an accomanying spouse or friend.

If a blind person is walking with you, don't grab his arm. Instead let him take your elbow if he chooses. Usually blind people will keep a half step behind you to anticipate curbs and steps.

If you know there is a blind person present when you walk into a room, speak as you enter. Introduce the blind person to others. Mention if there is a dog or a cat in the room. The possibility of a furry (albeit friendly!) creature springing into their lap is a very real one.

A partially opened door to a cabinet, a room, or a car can be a hazard to somebody who is blind. Be aware of situations that could cause accidents.

There is no need to panic the first time you eat with a visually impaired person. Blind people will not have trouble with ordinary table skills. But you may want to ask if they need "directions" regarding where bowls of food are placed. If food is already on their plate, describe where things are as on the face of a clock, such as, "The mashed potatoes are at two o'clock and the peas and carrots are at three." Blind people know their way around. Most will tell you if they need more assistance.

There is no need to avoid words like *look* or *see*. Blind people use those words too. Last week I had a conversation that went like this:

"Hi, it's nice to see you," I said to the blind woman who signed up for our luncheon.

"Nice to see you too," she replied, extending her hand.

I reached forward until my fingers touched hers. Immediately, she gave me a handshake. "It's a beautiful morning, isn't it?" I said, glancing out the restaurant window at the trees and flowers. "Has anyone described the view to you yet?"

"Not actually. What's going on outside?"

"There's a row of oleanders by the window and . . . yes, I even see a few birds making a nest."

"Really!" she exclaimed.

Before I knew it, the rest of the people seated at the table joined in our lively conversation.

Be sure to invite people with disabilities to events such as parties, concerts, and Bible studies. And offer to help them find a way for them to get there. While churches are opening their doors more and more, it won't mean much if they can't get there!

You can be of great assistance if you can do some work around the house. Ask a disabled person if they would like any help with cleaning, yard work, laundry, etc. You never want to ask as if they can't do those things, but you can phrase it diplomatically like "I've got hands I can offer if you need help with anything around the house. Don't be shy about asking. Name it and I'll help the best I can." A disabled person who has been taught well in their rehabilitation process will know just how to take you up on the offer.

Have a party, at their place! Suggest the idea of having a pot-luck supper with friends at their apartment or house. Bring over Laurel and Hardy movies and popcorn and laugh!

One friend we know has a plane. He and his friends took their disabled friend for a plane ride and an overnight retreat. The process of getting her into the plane was comical but the memories and friendships created were lasting.

Do You Get The Idea?

YOUR IMAGINATION CAN RUN wild with ideas for how to do friendship. Before running wild, however, keep these guidelines in mind:

1. Ask

Don't do anything (unless it's a surprise party) without first engaging in conversation with them. Recently, I was wheeling in an airport crosswalk, my lap and foot pedals loaded with luggage. A man ran up behind me, tucked his briefcase under his arm, and grabbed my wheelchair handles.

"Here, let me give you a hand," he shouted above the traffic as he threw his weight behind my chair. Before I could respond, the front wheels abruptly stopped against the lip of the curb, throwing me and my luggage forward.

Packages were scattered everywhere. The man scrambled to gather my things. "I'm so sorry . . . I'm so sorry."

I could tell his motive to help was sincere. But I warned him against future catastrophes, saying, "It's okay. Just make sure next time you ask before you act."

2. Follow through

More hurts have been felt because of well-meaning friends who told a disabled person they would do this or that. A shopping trip might be easy to cancel for you, but if it's the only trip the person will have gone on in three weeks and won't have a way of getting out for another two weeks, it can be disastrous.

3. Establish boundaries

A friendship with a person with a disability is not a contract. They are not a client of yours. Nor are you their employee. Be sure to communicate what you can't do as well as what you can do. If your disabled friend says, "Hey, can you take me to a doctor's appointment next week?" you should feel free to respond, "Great. But I should warn you, I can't do any lifting." Or you might say, "That depends. When is your appointment? I'm not available in the afternoons." *Whatever* limitation or question you have, say it.

4. Involve others in the friendship

The kind of friendship that provides a helping hand doesn't need to be done alone. The more the merrier—and the more the blessing gets passed around. One helpful book in this regard is *Circle of Friends* by Bob Perske. The book describes how people with disabilities can develop relationships with a small group of people to assist them with life issues such as transportation, housing, physical care, and so on. Though not written from a Christian perspective, his ideas seem to jump right out of the story of the four friends who helped the disabled friend down through the roof.

The Gift of Touch

TOUCHING SOMEONE WITH A disability may be a big step for many people. The sense of fear and discomfort might be highest in this regard. But people with disabilities, like all humans, need touch to affirm the existence of friendship and acceptance.

But what is appropriate touch?

When you encounter someone in a wheelchair for the first time, please don't casually put your foot up on the wheel or hang on the armrest. I don't know how to explain it other than to say that a wheelchair is part of a person's body space. Hanging or leaning on a wheelchair is similar to leaning on a person sitting in a chair. That kind of familiarity is reserved for close friends who find it comfortable to hug or embrace occasionally.

Don't feel shy about shaking the hand of a paralyzed person. One afternoon when my girlfriend and I were visiting a shopping mall, I noticed a large woman and a shorter man, arm in arm, walking toward me. As they drew nearer, the man's face brightened.

"Aren't you the lady who paints with her mouth?" he said as he extended his hand toward me.

"Why yes, I—"

"Don't do that!" the woman hoarsely whispered as she smacked his wrist. "Don't you know she can't feel?!"

"Please, I don't mind—," I began to say.

She jerked his elbow and pulled him away, shaking her finger. The man looked over his shoulder and meekly waved good-bye. I sighed and shrugged my shoulders. What could have been a pleasant exchange between the man and me was rudely aborted. If only the woman had approached our encounter with common sense. If it is natural for you to shake a person's hand, then feel free to shake the hand of a person who's in a wheelchair.

But, you may say, what if the person has a prosthetic arm such as a metal hook for a hand? Then feel free to shake his hook, especially if he extends the prosthesis toward you. Don't be concerned at grasping a piece of cold metal and giving it a pleasant shake—the disabled person considers that piece of metal his "hand." However, if you have second thoughts or feel too awkward, reach for his other hand or shoulder.

If the person is not capable of raising his paralyzed hand to you, go ahead and reach for it anyway, giving it a gentle squeeze. But I must underline the word "gentle." Some people struggle with painful arthritis in their hands.

Incidentally, people who are blind need you to take the initiative and reach out to them. Often they will extend a hand and expect you to respond.

Usually I lift my arm so people can shake my hand. I can't feel their grasp. My fingers cannot naturally intertwine with theirs. Sometimes they only hold my wrist. (Children shake my two fingers!) Whatever "handshake" method you choose, it is the gesture that counts, closing the distance between two people. Touching communicates acceptance and warmth.

When visiting someone at home or at a facility, don't be afraid to come close. I was so thankful for friends who would come visit me. When they walked into the room, I desperately wanted them to draw closer.

But sometimes people would merely pull up their chairs and sit no nearer than the foot of my bed. Others, who came with them, would linger in the doorway, leaning against the wall. I assured them that the nurses wouldn't mind if they sat on my bed. But most of those people stayed at an arm's length—or maybe two arms' lengths—from my shoulders. I say "shoulders" because that's where I could have felt their embrace if only they had reached out.

The degree to which you touch someone with a disability will depend upon your level of friendship. The guiding principle is not to cross boundaries of etiquette that you would not cross with a nondisabled person.

How Can I Give?

WE ARE A COUNTRY that likes to solve problems. And we often like to solve problems with "stuff." We are blessed with an abundance of material blessings here and God has graciously allowed us to give good "stuff" to people around the world.

Some creative thinking can be applied when communicating love to people with disabilities through giving. Many disabled people have a long list of things they need to help them live their lives. Vans might need a hydraulic lift. A computer might be needed to help them communicate. A specially designed wheelchair, costing over $10,000, is not an uncommon need for physically disabled people. Braille books for the blind and special phones for people who are deaf (Telecommunication Devices for the Deaf or TDD) are two more needed items. The list, as I said, can be long.

Though your resources might be limited and you may not be able to help with these kinds of items, there might be ways in which you can give unique and thoughtful gifts. Here's a sample shopping list:

For those in a rehabilitation hospital or a nursing home:

Pick up small pleasures like Snickers bars or cashews (if the doctor doesn't outlaw them!).

Bring by the latest magazines.

Give stationery to those who can write or offer to write letters for those who can't.

A good book or its audio version along with a tape player in case they don't have one.

A miniature Christmas tree if they are there during the holidays.

The list of ideas could go on. You get the idea.

For those with mental disabilities:

The temptation might be to give kid's stuff because they might have a comprehension level of a young child. And yet, a forty-five-year-old Down-syndrome man may dislike Barney as much as you do! Rather, give them a gift related to something they enjoy.

If that same man is a baseball fan, consider taking him to a ball game.

Games requiring complex analytical skills might be inap-
propriate so ask the person's parent or guardian what
games they enjoy.

Christian music is a wonderful way of sharing God's love
with a mentally disabled friend.

Clothing, pictures, a camera—the list is shortened only by the
ability of the person to whom you want to give the gift.

For a person who is blind:

Audio tapes of books, messages, and music.

Items of clothing that fit his or her perception of taste and
not your perception of what they ought to look like.

For a person with hearing impairments:

Videos with closed-captions or with a signer.

Books for those able to read.

Photos and photo albums.

The preceding lists are in no way meant to be exhaustive,
but I think they give you an idea of how to think about giving.
A little common sense mixed in with an understanding of the
other person's need.

Learn the Language

THE NUANCES OF THE language of love are as varied as the number of people that employ the language. Each receives love and
friendship differently. And each gives it differently. However you
choose to show your friendship, keep this abiding principle in
mind: Friendship's wealth is not found in the exchange of what
we own but in the emptying of ourselves. You can love best with
what is most important to the other person—yourself.

SEVEN

God's Friendliest Church

REMEMBER A MORNING WHEN you just wanted to stay in bed? For me, Sundays are tough. In fact, one Sunday I wrestled to bring my emotions firmly in line with my will just so I could face the morning.

By the time Ken and I arrived at church and settled in, I was looking forward to the service. As the choir sang the opening hymn, one of the ushers wheeled in a young man from a local nursing home. He was new to church. The usher parked his wheelchair directly in front of me. The young man's arms were very spastic as he tried to hold onto the hymnal, and I wished someone in the pew would slide over to help.

My eyes were drawn to the back of his chair where a word board dangled from one of the handles. It was lopsided, but I could read a few of the sentences on the board. A block of sentences were grouped together, listing weekly activities:

Please take me to therapy.
Please wheel me to the lunch room.
Please take me to occupational therapy.
I need to see a nurse.
I need to go to the bathroom.

This was how the man communicated with his friends during the course of the week. He would obviously point to the particular sentence which best expressed his need.

Another list seemed to be for weekend routines. I was struck by the last sentence.

Please let me have a pizza.
I want to go out to a ball game.
Please take me to a movie.
Please take me to church.

Here's the point. I'm sure that disabled man faces his share of Sunday mornings when he doesn't feel like getting up. Yet despite the difficulties of finding a staff person in the nursing home to help him arise extra early, he still wanted to be in church. It heartened me to picture him pointing to a sentence scrawled on a word board that said, "Please take me to church."

At that point my emotions immediately lined themselves up with my will. Suddenly I was happy. I was happy to be in church and fellowshipping with this young man who said, "Please . . . please take me to church."

He couldn't have realized how the Lord used him to encourage me. By his mere presence, my attitude had changed from "grit-my-teeth-and-bear-it" to heartfelt joy and praise to God. Without realizing it, he was demonstrating the biblical injunction from 1 Thessalonians 5:11 to "encourage one another and build each other up."

Making the Disabled Feel Welcome

I ONCE ASKED DR. J. I. Packer, an outstanding theologian and author, what advice he might give to a Christian disabled person who was relegated to a back bedroom, away from Christian friends. What value does such a person have in the kingdom of Christ?

His answer would give worth even to the most severely disabled individual. "God doesn't want us for the sake of the things we can do for him. He wants our love. He wants our fellowship. He wants our worship. And any of us—rich or poor, healthy or ill—can offer him this."

The disabled are particularly aware of being judged by their abilities and accomplishments ... or lack of them. It is in God's economy that the disabled person finds acceptance and love just because of who she is, not because of what she can do.

The church is to be a reality of that approval. Perhaps that is why we are told in Hebrews, "Let us not give up meeting together, as some are in the habit of doing, but let us encourage one another." There are no exceptions. We are all to come together, able-bodied and disabled alike.

No one is to be set apart. As much as possible, a handicapped person should have the opportunity to get involved with able-bodied people, to share, to worship with them. Sitting side-by-side in pews, their voices can unite in praise.

"Special sections" off to the side for people in wheelchairs may tend to foster even more separation. (Even a section for the deaf can be more centrally located near the front of the church so the pastor's expressions are more visible.) It should be added, though, that some mentally retarded individuals may appreciate a worship service of their own, better designed to meet their interest level and attention span.

But the rule of thumb should be involvement. Singing together, sitting near one another, touching, and being face-to-face has a way of breaking down barriers of fear and ignorance. Being one. That is what the body of Christ is all about.

I often refer to 1 Corinthians 12:14–23 when I encourage integration among the able-bodied and disabled: "Now the body is not made up of one part but of many.... God has arranged the parts in the body, every one of them, just as he wanted them to be.... The eye cannot say to the hand, 'I don't need you!' And the head cannot say to the feet, 'I don't need you!' On the contrary, those parts of the body that seem to be weaker are indispensable, and the parts that we think are less honorable we treat with special honor."

Do we honestly see the disabled as indispensable in our church?

Let me share a personal illustration. My hands, though paralyzed and without feeling, are indispensable to me. They are definitely the weakest members of my body. That is hard for some people to understand because they see photographs of me gesturing. It appears that I'm using my hands.

It sure looks like that, but let me explain. I have very strong shoulder muscles and fairly strong biceps. With those muscles I can flail my arms around. That makes my fingers and hands flop about. But I have absolutely no muscles from my elbows down. It only looks like I do.

Yet although my hands and fingers are lifeless, they are not useless. With the aid of a special arm splint I am able to feed myself. When I drive, my hand rests in a handcuff attached to the steering column so I can brake and accelerate. My fingers can't turn pages, but with upper-arm muscles I am able to nudge them underneath a page and flip it over.

My hands and fingers, though lifeless and paralyzed, are so very useful!

Do you see the parallel? In that same chapter of 1 Corinthians it says, "Now you are the body of Christ and each one of you is a part of it" (v. 27). That includes your disabled friend—who, by the world's standards, seems so ineffective, totally unable to accomplish any real good for the rest of the fellowship.

It isn't that way. God says the weaker members are indispensable. The Body is not complete without them. And with a bit of creativity and help from the stronger members of the fellowship, they can make a difference ... and they do.

I wish all churches viewed disabled people that way. Unfortunately, there are more than 43 million disabled people living in the United States, but far too few churches have regular ministries to reach out to them.

We can change that statistic! As the disabled are accepted into Christ's church, they will want to become actively involved. Here are a few practical ways we can help handicapped people feel welcome, as suggested by the Christian League for the Handicapped:

> Get acquainted with at least one handicapped person in your church. That means more than a "Good morning ... nice to see you ... have a nice day." Spend an extended period of time with him. Although it's important, Sunday morning conversation is often too hurried and interrupted to be more than superficial.
>
> Be aware of families with disabled children. It may be difficult for the parents to find experienced baby-sitters and they might be having a difficult time in getting to church because of that.
>
> Offer to hold a hymnbook or look up Bible passages for a disabled person. Suggest to your Bible study group to take on a love project for a disabled individual.

Acts of kindness such as these will make a disabled person or the family much more welcome at church.

Making Your Church Ready

CAN YOUR PHYSICALLY DISABLED friend even get through your church door? If not, it could be a little embarrassing.

I will never forget the time I went shopping at a local mall with a couple friends. In one of the stores we found a pile of pretty sweaters on a clearance table. Wanting to try on a few items, we grabbed the sweaters and headed for the ladies' dressing room.

I maneuvered my power wheelchair through the door of the dressing room, but before I knew it, I was stuck in the narrow aisle. I couldn't inch forward or backward.

Worse yet, several other women in the dressing room got stuck too—I was blocking them in. There was no way for them to get out, except by climbing over me—and they weren't the type of women to do that. There I sat, unable to say anything cute and clever. I felt horrible—the women probably had schedules to meet and appointments to keep.

What a traffic hazard! The manager, along with the store clerk, pushed and pulled my wheelchair until finally it unwedged. I was embarrassed. (The manager was even more embarrassed. He promised to make room for wheelchairs!) I learned an important lesson, though. Always check the accessibility of any dressing room before I agree to try on clothes!

I giggle when I think of that incident. But I wasn't giggling when it happened. These situations happen to the disabled more than any of us would think.

Thankfully, more is being done all the time to remove existing architectural barriers, and many architects of public buildings and malls have planned their new structures with an awareness for the handicapped.

But the church, for some reason, has lagged behind in providing accessibility. Many assume that the ADA brought on major changes for buildings. Unfortunately, churches were excluded from having to comply with the ADA so there is no legal motivation to make changes. So double-check your church building. If there are too many architectural roadblocks to overcome, your friend may feel like her presence just isn't all that important to the church.

Accessibility means far more than wide doorways and ramps. See your church through the eyes of a disabled person.

Are you truly putting out "welcome" signs? Are you getting the message across, "Hello! Come on in! We've prepared a place for you and we want you to feel right at home"?

No doubt your church already has some welcome signs. Ringing bells and open doors, smiling ushers and firm handshakes are a great start.

But there are other creative ways to welcome the disabled. A close and designated parking area for people in wheelchairs says "welcome" loudly and clearly. A curb cut will communicate, "We've taken the time to think ahead. We've done something about these obstacles to make it easier for you to fellowship here."

Walk through your church building with a physically handicapped friend. Take notes as he points out possible changes that would make it easier to get around. Lowered water fountains. Bathrooms with wide alcoves and grab bars. A portion of a pew removed so a wheelchair does not block an aisle. Blocks of wood which can be wedged under the front wheels of a chair that is parked on a slant.

Making a church accessible is not easy. And it can be expensive. But we're not talking about making major structural changes immediately. The important thing is that you lay out the "welcome mat," at least making it possible for a wheelchair to get from the parking lot to the sanctuary without having to be carried up a flight of stairs.

The hearing impaired could use amplifying devices that can be hooked into several pews. Is there sufficient lighting in the sanctuary for the hearing impaired? It is difficult for them to read lips or to see signing if the lighting is poor. If your church has a ministry with hearing impaired, consider installing a TDD (telecommunication device for the deaf) so they can call the church.

The visually impaired will know they are welcomed when they see large print hymnbooks and Bibles. And what a vital ministry for the blind if someone would braille the hymns and the sermon text each week. There is no doubt about that welcome!

Even more important than these architectural welcome mats is the attitude of God's people. Jesus understood this. In Luke 14 he told the story of a man who had a great banquet and invited many guests. Now it is hard to imagine, but these friends found excuses to do anything but eat! They had fields to attend to, oxen to try out, and a new wife—maybe good excuses, but it angered the master that other things were more important to them than his banquet. So he ordered the servant, "Go out quickly into the streets and alleys of the town and bring in the poor, the crippled, the blind, and the lame. . . . Go out to the roads and country lanes and make them come in, so that my house will be full."

Notice the insistence in the master's command—"bring them in" . . . "make them come in." Does your disabled friend sense this kind of urgency in your invitation to come to church? Or is it a kind of off-the-cuff, "Uh, by the way, uh, if you don't have anything better to do on Sunday, why don't you see if you can come to church."

We are to bring them in, "make" them come. Now I'm not telling you to drag your disabled friend, against his will, to church next Sunday. Let me explain. After living with the demands of a physical limitation all week, most handicapped people are worn out by Sunday. They simply lack the emotional stamina, the initiative, to attend church. They spend Monday through Friday arranging attendant care, shopping, doctor visits, and housekeeping. The last thing they may want to do is ask one more person for a ride to church. It is easier to stay home and watch church on television.

Take my friend Debbie. She is in a wheelchair and has a speech impediment. She takes the bus during the week but must find other transportation on Sundays. Every Saturday afternoon she would have to make the rounds of phoning different people for a ride. Her wheelchair eliminated drivers who have small sporty cars. Then she had to cross off her list people with bad backs. And she also avoided asking people who had trouble accepting her deformities. She didn't want to make them ill at ease.

Now, my friend Debbie is a particularly persevering sort. But the truth is most disabled people will not dig in their heels and persevere when it comes to arranging their own transportation to church services. Although the people they ask usually have valid reasons for not providing rides, the average disabled person tends to interpret a "no" answer as a personal rejection.

Finding it difficult to get a ride to church suggests that they are unwanted. And once the disabled person feels rejected by a congregation, the next thought may be that God doesn't want disabled people either.

Our responsibility is clear. We must take the initiative to get handicapped people to church. Invite, yes. But we must go beyond that. Like the story in Luke 14, we must bring them.

Evangelizing Your Disabled Friend

WHEN I WAS IN the hospital, I dreaded people who would come into my ward prepared to announce the gospel to me. And I don't use that word "announce" lightly. I am sure they had a definite notion of how the conversation would go. Maybe some of those people assumed I would ask the standard questions. In their minds, they had standard answers.

Looking back, I wish those conversations could have been more successful. One problem was that those people were more concerned about imposing their faith, rather than exposing it. Yet even now, years later, I fall into the same trap when I talk about Jesus to friends or neighbors who don't know him. I impose rather than expose my faith.

Perhaps you have done the same. Jesus has made a differ-ence in your life, and you are convinced he will do the same for your disabled friend. You mechanically recite salvation verses, praying all the while that you won't forget anything. But your friend seems unmoved. You can't help but be depressed by her rejection of Christ.

The truth is, we cannot make someone a Christian. We must let our faith be known, but we cannot dump it on others. In fact, if we aggressively throw our spiritual weight around, it could indicate our misunderstanding of the role of the Holy Spirit. We cannot convert anyone. Only the Spirit of Christ can do that.

That should give us comfort when it comes to giving the gospel to someone who, let's say, has just learned that his dis-ability is permanent.

Forget imposing your faith on your disabled friend. To expose your faith is so much easier ... and so much more nat-ural. There is nothing threatening or intimidating about getting into an honest conversation about God and what he means to you. It can be winsome and persuasive to casually share the real-ity of God in your everyday life.

Openness is appealing. Don't be afraid to ask leading ques-tions. And don't get defensive. You are not on the attack. You are simply opening up your life. You are letting another person see, in the most natural way, what makes you care, love, and give. It can be intimidating to share Christ with someone who just broke her neck in an automobile accident or a person whose disability is causing him further physical problems. In fact, this conversation happened very recently.

" ... And that's why I believe in God," I said as I leaned back in my wheelchair, letting my words sink into the thinking of the young man with post-polio syndrome. I didn't have to wait long.

"Don't talk to me about a good God. If he was so good, he would have never let this happen to me." The tone of his voice was soft as though he sincerely did not understand.

It was a delicate moment, so I waited before responding.

Finally, I continued, "Yeah, I know exactly how you feel. I've been there. Lying in a hospital bed with tubes running in and out of you tends to throw out of focus any preconceived notions of a good God. And from a human point of view, God certainly doesn't look very good, does he?"

The man looked a little stunned, surprised even. I had thrown back at him his hot-potato question. He didn't know what to do with his argument. I could tell he was wondering why I, a Christian, would agree with him that God doesn't look very fair. "Uh . . . no, he doesn't look fair. . . . Listen, are you playing some sort of game?" he said, squinting his eyes.

"Not at all. I'm just being truthful. From an earthly point of view, God doesn't come out smelling like a rose when it comes to human suffering." I could tell the hot potato was cooling a bit.

He looked me straight in the eyes, his expression more relaxed. As I watched the wheels turn in his head, I realized how explosive emotions dissipate when you deflect them with a little common sense.

Finally he spoke. "So . . . run by me one more time that stuff about a heavenly point of view." From there the discussion was no longer angry but sincerely earnest. I shared a heavenly, biblical perspective about his disability. It was his first step to eventually accepting Christ.

You may have to juggle a few hot-potato questions from your disabled friend—especially if he doesn't know Christ. Your friend will listen if you use careful common sense in handling God's Word.

These very people who have suffered are special objects of God's care and concern. In Revelation 3 Jesus says that he wishes people were either cold or hot. It grieves him that so many are lukewarm about spiritual things. Most disabled people I know are definitely not lukewarm!

Heavy-duty suffering has a way of pressing people up against spiritual walls. They are either hot, super interested in things in the Bible, or they are ice cold, calloused, and indifferent toward a life in Christ.

But, look! Jesus says that's a good place to be.

So don't let fear or intimidation overcome you when faced with an opportunity to share the gospel with someone who is disabled. After all, the Spirit is probably doing double duty in the life of a person backed into spiritual corners. It is the Spirit who has prepared the other person's heart, and it is the Spirit who will give you the natural and supernatural words to say. It may be that you were brought into his life for such a time as this!

Being on the Giving End

AFTER I LEFT THE hospital, finally drawing closer to Christ, I read 1 Corinthians 3:11–13, "For no one can lay any foundation other than the one already laid, which is Jesus Christ. If any man builds on this foundation using gold, silver, costly stones . . . his work will be shown for what it is." That hospital experience was God's way of laying my foundation bare. Now he was ready to begin the slow process of cementing into my character gold and silver. I had to learn to be a servant. I had to start to be on the giving end.

Eight long years passed and finally I was able to catalog my journey in the book *Joni*. I guess I would have been content after the book came out to remain on the farm and continue to paint. But opportunities kept coming: other books, chances to travel, a movie, a record. And God was building into my life a deeper love of Jesus and a desire to help others reach their full spiritual maturity in Christ.

Books and speaking engagements have little to do, though, with the silver and costly stones talked about in 1 Corinthians

3. Popularity and prestige carry little weight with God. For that matter, most disabled people don't have the chance to give their testimony at a Christian women's club, much less put it all down in a book. But the success of what a disabled person builds on his foundation is measured by the gold of obedience, the silver of a refined faith, and the precious gems of loyalty and faithfulness as he serves others by exercising his unique spiritual gift.

Disabled People Also Have Gifts

FIRST PETER 4:10–11 SAYS, "Each one should use whatever gift he has received to serve others, faithfully administering God's grace in its various forms. If anyone speaks, he should do it as one speaking the very words of God. If anyone serves, he should do it with the strength God provides, so that in all things God may be praised through Jesus Christ." This verse doesn't apply to only the able-bodied. It is for the disabled too. We all have gifts of the Spirit.

May I encourage you to help your disabled friend discover his spiritual gift? Would you help him find a niche in your church where he can exercise his gift? For openers, look through the list of gifts in Romans 12:6–8. What area of service listed there gives your disabled friend the most joy? Encourage him to use his gift, praying for wisdom and direction. Perhaps he will find a place to serve where no one else is meeting the need. (Your church may have to accommodate the limitations of your disabled friend, forgetting how "things have always been done" in the past.)

Don't let the disability stand in the way of service. My friend Bonnie has MS and is in a wheelchair. She teaches a lively class of second graders. Those children learn about Jesus while gaining handicap awareness—all at the same time. And Bonnie's right at their eye level!

Team teaching is a good idea if your friend has the gift of teaching yet has limitations. Results do not depend on how well a teacher passes out books, collects papers, or sharpens pencils. Your disabled friend can borrow someone's hands to do those tasks, while she devotes herself to teaching. The results, then, depend on the Spirit. First Corinthians 2:2–5 says, "For I resolved to know nothing while I was with you except Jesus Christ and him crucified. I came to you in weakness and fear, and with much trembling. My message and my preaching were not with wise and persuasive words, but with a demonstration of the Spirit's power, so that your faith might not rest on men's wisdom, but on God's power."

Leadership responsibilities in the church can't be overlooked. There are gifted people being overlooked regularly just because they are disabled. If you sense that your friend has the gift of leadership or administration, encourage them and also serve as an advocate for the church to consider that person for a leadership role. There are too many examples in history of people with disabilities playing vital leadership roles. President Roosevelt looms as the most prominent world leader with a disability.

Kathleen M. Muldoon in her *Finger, Toe and Lip Service* catalogued a number of ways that disabled Christians exercise their gifts in the church. The list may give you other ideas on how the disabled in your congregation can use their Spirit-given spiritual gifts.

A ministry of prayer

There are often prayer chains, groups, or cells within the church. For the severely disabled person who may not be able to even leave his hospital bed or home, there can be a powerful ministry of prayer. He can intercede for the needs of his friends, family, and church. I know of a disabled person who is a personal prayer partner of a college and career pastor—he receives an updated list of the names and needs of young people in the church. When people in the congregation become aware of this ministry, there will be no lack of petitions!

Prayer can be an international ministry. The disabled person can pray for missionaries around the world and for religious and national leaders. It is no small task to pray for food for the starving, protection for the persecuted, and the many other petitions that the Spirit reminds him of as he hears the news of the world and nation.

A mail ministry

There is nothing like receiving a note of encouragement from someone. A mail ministry is one way to build others up in the faith, deepen friendships, encourage those who are ill, and share meaningful Scriptures.

You can assist your friend in a mail ministry by offering your hands if they are unable to write. Offer to operate a tape recorder for them as they "talk" a letter.

Disabled people can reach out to those who many others do not have time for. Think of prisoners who go months without receiving mail; people in convalescent homes who look for letters in their mailbox; or people in hospitals who would appreciate a get-well card. And it can mean so much to people in a rehab center who need a reminder that there are brighter days ahead! Your pastor most likely knows of shut-ins who have little contact with the outside world and would cherish a note. And missionaries spend much of their time writing letters and yet receive very few in return.

As with the prayer ministry, the Lord will bring to mind those who need this kind of encouragement. In these areas, the disabled can shine.

A telephone ministry

"Reach out and touch someone" is far more than just a catchy telephone ad. It is something that the disabled can do from their own homes for the good of the body of Christ. Many elderly people long for the opportunity to talk to someone—to know that there is someone who cares about them, who will ask about their family, who will allow them to reminisce. A telephone ministry may involve "checking up" on the needs of people who have little contact with others during the week.

A creative friend of Kathleen Muldoon has a ministry to children in her church. She put a note in the bulletin and asked for parents to contact her if they were interested in her calling their children when they arrived home from school. What started as just a "check-in call" has developed into friendships with the children. They pray together. She even helps them with occasional problems. This disabled person is someone very special to each of those kids.

My friend Diane, who uses a handicap-adapted phone, is responsible to telephone disabled people who sign up for transportation to our church during the week. She has developed a network that links drivers with people who need rides.

The opportunities to minister, using the gifts God has given, are unlimited. God has made us each uniquely in his image. Our gifts are unique. And our opportunities to use those gifts in his kingdom are unique. That should make each one of us sense the urgency of serving him—in our own way, in the place he has put us, using the gifts he has given us. It is an awesome privilege.

Is Your Church Friendly?

HERE'S A HANDY SET of questions to ask your church about its friendliness toward people with disabilities.

Is our building friendly?

Plenty of reserved parking spaces on level ground, close to the entrances. Easy entrance into the building.

Accessible restrooms.

Good seating locations in the sanctuary that don't isolate people.

Accessibility to all parts of the building, not just the sanctuary.

Are the ushers and greeters friendly?

Do they make good eye contact with everyone?

Do they ask questions about where a person with a disability wants to sit?

Do they offer services or information to assist a disabled visitor?

Are the programs of the church friendly?

Large print bulletins and Bibles available.

Hearing "loops" available for those with hearing impairments.

Respite care for kids with disabilities during worship service.

Opportunities for kids to be integrated into regular Sunday school classes if desired.

Transportation to get people to church.

A tape ministry of the Sunday service for people in nursing homes.

Invitations extended to everyone to participate in social activities.

How friendly are the people?

Does our church leadership have a clear perspective on what God says about people with disabilities?

Does the church's mission seek to include people with disabilities?

Are people in the church aware of the needs of disabled people as well as what they have to offer the church?
When someone with a disability does attend our church, what is the response of the congregation?

The Next Steps

A CHURCH WITH AN active disability ministry is a joy to the heart of Jesus. Even more joyous is when it seems to be not a ministry but rather a way of life. But how can you get started?

JAF Ministries has a number of resources available to get a ministry started and to keep it growing.

A Disability Awareness Sunday Kit

This kit comes complete with a program for your Sunday school as well as for the worship service. It's a great way to raise the awareness of people in your church and to recruit folks who want to start a formal ministry.

How to Create an Effective Disability Outreach

This self-paced guide comes with training materials, a video, and instructions on how to recruit people, how to plan, and how to publicize your ministry.

All God's Children

This book describes ministry ideas for each type of disability.

That All May Worship

This publication was developed by the National Organization on Disability. It gives excellent ideas for making program and architectural changes to enhance ministry to people with disabilities.

There are many general resources like these in addition to those dealing with more specific topics available through JAF Ministries. Feel free to contact the ministry at the address given at the end of the book for information on how you can turn your church into a place of joy for people with disabilities in your community.

Part Three

It's a Two-Way Street

EIGHT

Eye-to-Eye

GEORGE GENTRY JUST STOPPED by my office for a visit. It's a treat whenever I have a chance to talk with this paraplegic friend who was disabled in Vietnam. His smile is warm, his eyes are bright, and his voice is soft. But today, as we chatted about Medicaid cutbacks and the new Disability Rights Center in Washington, I found myself thinking, *Why do I enjoy being with this guy so much?*

The answer came the next second. In fact, I smiled and said, "George, you are one of the few people with whom I see things eye-to-eye. Literally." It was a joke and he laughed. But we knew it went deeper than that.

For one thing, George and I are both veterans. No, I don't mean of the Vietnam sort, but of a rigorous and demanding life of paralysis. We were both spinal cord injured in 1967. And although we are never nostalgic about our "war stories in wheelchairs," George and I understand the bond between us. I may be much closer to other people, my husband included, but spinal-cord-injured friends like the two of us have a special connection. We have been through—and we are still going through—something we don't share with just any person off the street.

For the last seven chapters I have been talking to parents and advocates, husbands, wives, and siblings of people affected by everything from osteogenesis-imperfecta to stroke. This chapter and the next are different. You are the one who just stopped by my office for a visit. You and I share the same thing. We have a disability.

If we were together, I would want to talk about the same bond you, George, and I share together. That is why this chapter is less about information and more about strengthening that bond. It's about understanding those times when the disability not only spins out of control, rips into your sanity, and tears apart your body, but more importantly, it's about the times when the disability can become the Jacob's ladder on which you rise to new levels of hope and purpose.

If You Could Change the Way Things Are ... Would You?

No THINKING PERSON CHOOSES suffering. In fact, if I had a choice, I might opt to be a paraplegic like George. *Really?* I can hear you saying. *But, Joni, in your photos you look like you have it all together.* Yeah, right! Chalk it up to good back lighting. Quadriplegia, whether on or off camera, isn't easy.

Not that George has it easy. But the difference a few millimeters in a spinal cord injury makes is incredible. He has hands; I don't. And that makes all the difference in the world. I would love to be able to grab hand-rims on a manual wheelchair and give a good shove. It would be great to comb my hair. Or empty my leg bag. And I am not even counting fun stuff like plucking guitar strings with my fingers, jogging till my muscles burn, or soaking in a hot tub under vanilla-scented bubbles.

I don't want to start a pity party, but may I let you in on a few other struggles? Like when I wake up at 4:30 A.M. with my arm killing me from lying in one position all night. I glance at the clock. Ken's alarm is set for 5:30 A.M. The "caring wife" side of me insists he get his full night's sleep. The other side, the hurting part, groans to call for help. By the time I have wrestled over what to do, I am wide awake. So usually, I will wriggle my shoulder into a more comfortable position and try to get back to sleep. It doesn't always happen. That is when mad middle-of-the-night moments have me wishing I were able-bodied.

Then there was the time my batteries gave out at the Topanga Plaza Mall. Without a friend nearby, I had to flag down a passer-by to push me to a public phone, reach in my wallet, get a quarter, and dial my husband for help (thankfully he was home!). It is hard when your hands don't work.

Other uncomfortable and inconvenient areas come into my mind. Training new personal-care attendants and exposing a stranger to the privacy of my bedroom. Flipping through lingerie catalogs and envying the shapes of bodies beautiful (come to think of it, 95 percent of women probably struggle with that). Reading *Managing Incontinence* over the weekend when I would rather be immersed in *Time* magazine or *Bed and Bath Remodeling*.

What hurts most is the occasional loneliness that hollows out my heart. It comes from always sitting down in a standing-up world. People do their best to fill the hole, but sometimes it's as though a thin pane of glass separates me from my friends, even my closest ones. I am sure this is another reason why it was pleasant to be with George Gentry today.

Paralyzed life for paras or quads isn't easy.

So for a moment, let's peel back our defenses and confess how we both would rather leapfrog all the baggage that goes with our disabilities. How we would like to detour the distress and shortcut the suffering. Let's ask ourselves, "If we could change this, would we?"

I thought about this question during my talk with George. We were discussing the controversy surrounding a statue they want to sculpt of Franklin D. Roosevelt. One camp is saying, "Don't show him as disabled. Leave the wheelchair out of the final sculpture!" The other is saying, "Don't be embarrassed. Show him with his crutches or his chair. It's a part of who Roosevelt was!"

George asked my opinion. I was quick to respond: "Roosevelt was a gutsy, go-for-it leader who inspired people up and out of the Great Depression. He may not have realized it at the time, but I'll bet anything that *chutzpah* was forged by his disability. Anyway, I'll go for the biblical perspective that says, 'glory in the infirmity and boast in the weakness.'"

As you might suspect, I wouldn't change a thing. And if given the option, at this point I wouldn't prefer paraplegia (promise you won't hold me to this when I am having a horrid day of "sweats" or "flushes" or if I am the first in line for a breakthrough cure!). All things considered, I would stick with my disability. If they ever made a statue of me, I would want my 300-pound Everest & Jennings power chair front and center.

It Hasn't Always Been This Way

"I AM THE VICTIM of a terrible diving accident," I said in a flat and factual way to the lawyer. "It has left me completely paralyzed from the shoulders down."

My dad's lawyer quietly jotted copious notes as I droned on. I was numb and hurting; I didn't flinch at all at the idea of making Maryland Beach, Inc., pay. As far as I was concerned, it was their fault the water was too shallow.

I thought my diving accident was everybody's fault. I wanted everyone to pay. The Department of Vocational Rehabilitation owed me a good case manager. My church (which I really wasn't involved much with back then) should help. After all, that is what churches were supposed to do; I was a victim of an awful tragedy. I *really* pushed this victimization thing on my parents: "You were the ones who brought me into this world. It's all your fault, Mom and Dad!"

Looking back, I am certain that most of my anger and depression was rooted in the "victim thing." People in our culture of comfort feel swindled by life. People are victims of diving accidents, drunk drivers, and polio epidemics. And not just as it relates to a disability. People feel victimized in their marriages or by abusive childhoods, violent crime, or discrimination. Many have convinced themselves that someone else should either pay for the damages owed them or take responsibility for their lives. People who choose to see themselves as victims are those who choose self-pity.

I dug in for the long haul. Not only with a court case that seemed to drag on forever but with a cloud of deep depression. Frankly, after only a year of adjusting to life in a wheelchair, I began to tire of the self-pity. When I turned to the Bible, God's Spirit and a Christian friend named Steve Estes became my guides.

"Look," I said to Steve, "there's no way I can face a life of total paralysis with a happy attitude. It's just too much, too big."

He had a wise and ready reply: "I couldn't agree more. It is too much to ask. And God doesn't ask it of you either. He only asks you to take one day at a time."

This simply wasn't a pious platitude plucked off a cross-stitched plaque; this was a powerful and fundamental signpost from Scripture pointing to the path away from pain. I began to "wheel" the path starting with Lamentations 3:22–23, "Because of the Lord's great love we are not consumed, for his compassions never fail. They are new every morning; great is your faithfulness." I quickly learned this was the only way to live: one day at a time with God's enabling.

As I wheeled into my future one day at a time, I discovered other signposts from Scripture: "And we know that in *all* things God works for the good of those who love him . . ." and "In him we were also chosen . . . according to the plan of him who works *everything* in conformity with the purpose of his will." Dorothy Sayers echoed these signposts when she wrote that "God reaches down into what otherwise would be awful evil and wrenches out of it positive good for us and glory for himself."

Do these Bible verses sound like platitudes? I realize there are many people in the disability community who would like to confine the subject of God to the hospital chapel. But let's be honest—God and the Bible are as commonplace in rehab centers as bedpans and bottles of pills.

So, let's have a quick rehab lesson here. Traditional rehabilitation philosophy will pull out all the stops to address a patient's physical, psychological, emotional, and vocational needs, while spiritual needs are at best ignored. But more professionals are beginning to see that the rehabilitation of a person's spirit is key in affecting all those other areas. A healthy and whole spirit affects everything. Why? Because how a person relates to God has a profound influence on what he thinks about himself, his goals, and his friends and family.

A disabled person who connects with God usually demonstrates personal freedom, responsibility to the community, true achievement, and meaningful relationships with people. And what if a person gets overwhelmed by the "disability baggage" and ignores God, setting himself up at the center of his own moral universe? Well, those who remain masters of their own lives, to the exclusion of God and others, will inevitably negate themselves. As the Vatican papers have stated, "Man, who is alienated from the Source of Life, his Creator, expresses his dominion over his own life by destroying it."

I have seen this happen. I have seen people with multiple sclerosis or spinal cord injury at first become hopeful. When the prognosis doesn't change, they become sullen. Bargaining with God and with others perks them up for a while, but then anger settles in. Finally they play out the prediction of Hebrews 12:15 that warns, "See to it that no one misses the grace of God and that no bitter root grows up to cause trouble and defile many." I have seen people with disabilities spit venom at those they love, as well as drink the poison of bitterness and resentment themselves.

It hurts. Perhaps you have been there. And maybe, just maybe, you are *still* there.

Respond to the Grace of God

REMEMBER MY BLUBBERING TO my dad's lawyer about my anger against the owners of the beach where I broke my neck? We never won that court case. The truth is, I made a stupid, reckless dive. It was the truth that set me free, along with other truths like leaning daily on God's grace. Most of all, I discovered that playing the victim role is not consistent with living for Jesus Christ.

The irony is that you can't *imagine* a more victimized person than Jesus. The Scriptures tell us he had no real home. His friends were, for the most part, the fair-weather sort. He was brought like a lamb to the slaughter. He was betrayed and unjustly crucified, suffering a death he did not deserve. Yet when he died, he did not say "*I* am finished," but "*It* is finished." He did not play the victim and thus he emerged as the victor; and it is *this* example he has set for us.

Forget the self-pity. True, your circumstances might be downright awful. You might be living below the poverty level and inching by on Medicaid and Social Security. Your husband may be fed up with having to turn you at night. The help you hire doesn't stick around long and you are sick of training a new attendant for the umpteenth time. And, yes, you wish they would quit sending you those stupid lingerie catalogs.

Life itself is one big hardship. But remember, everything that touches the lives of God's children, he permits. This means victory is ours in Christ. It also means you can delete the word "victim" from your vocabulary. People who survive accidents or illnesses are just that: survivors. You are not a polio victim; you are a polio survivor. You are not victimized by multiple sclerosis, you are surviving it. The words that lift people up out of crisis are never words of defeat, but of hope and love (the love of God who knows, first hand, what it means to lose a family member in a tragedy).

So don't let go of hope. The prognosis may not change, but hope doesn't have to disappoint. The Bible says so in Romans 5:5. It also says that his grace (that is, the desire and the power to do his will) is enough to see you through. And just to make certain you have enough "reasons for going on," the Bible even says your disability has a purpose.

There Are No Accidents in a Christian's Life

I SAW BARBARA WALTERS' interview the other evening with Christopher Reeve, the *Superman* actor who became a quadriplegic in a horseback riding accident. I was inspired by his attitude and determination. I thought it was curious when he said, "I've got to believe there's a reason this has happened to me." If one carries out his statement to a logical conclusion, one must also believe that there exists a personal God who is the Designer behind the "reasons." Otherwise, Christopher's statement is just a nostalgic sentimentality.

This is why the Good News of the Bible is great news for people with impairments. God has designed reasons behind your disability. Good ones. A couple of pages ago I mentioned Romans 8:28 and Ephesians 1:11, "And we know that in *all things* God works for the good of those who love him ..." (italics mine) and "In him we were also chosen ... according to the plan of him who works *everything* in conformity with the purpose of his will (italics mine)." God, according to his will, works even bad things like spinal cord injury and multiple sclerosis together for good purposes. And learning some of these purposes sure does help. God's plan is for you to ...

Learn dependence. Learning to depend on other people for help teaches me how to lean on God. If I were completely self-sufficient, I wouldn't be aware of my desperate need of God. Able-bodied people may forget this reality, but people like you and me can't. We need God.

Learn contentment. True contentment comes when a person, no matter what his circumstances, is satisfied with the sufficiency of Christ. Like the apostle Paul says in Philippians 4:12–13, "I know what it is to be in need, and I know what it is to have plenty. I have learned the secret of being content in any and every situation. ... I can do everything through him who gives me strength." I can't tell you how good it feels to have a settled soul, even when I am "in need" such as those times when I'm bedridden with pressure sores.

Receive God's power. The apostle Paul went to God for help in his disability, "But he said to me, 'My grace is sufficient for you, for my power is made perfect in weakness.'" There is not a committed Christian who doesn't desire God's power to flow through his life. However, God's power at its best is only manifested through a believer who acknowledges his weaknesses. This means you and I have an advantage over many others—our weaknesses are built-in!

Boast in your weaknesses. God is not the sort of father who wants his children to grow up, leave the nest, and "get out there on your own!" Rather, he desires that we always stay "close to home" so that he can shelter, protect, and provide. So go ahead and boast in the built-in weakness of your disability! The more you boast of your need of God, the more you avail yourself of his power.

Experience God deeply. Keeping in mind Paul's disability, listen to what he writes in Philippians 3:8, 10: "I consider everything a loss compared to the surpassing greatness of knowing Christ Jesus, my Lord, for whose sake I have lost all things. . . . I want to know Christ and the power of his resurrection and the fellowship of sharing in his sufferings." What have you lost? Use of your legs? Twenty-twenty vision? A mind that thinks clearly? The greatest good your loss will gain you is an increased capacity in your soul for God. Your handicapping condition is a kind of passport into the fellowship of sharing in Christ's sufferings—a circle in which you will better identify with your Savior, as well as experience a greater release of faith and understanding.

Be a witness. Your wheelchair, white cane, or walker can be a pulpit. First, just as everyone notices a pulpit behind which a minister speaks, others cannot help but notice your weaknesses. Plus, the idea of a pulpit carries with it credibility and authority. When you develop a godly response to your wheelchair, you will have developed a powerful life message; with your greater limitations, you can teach those with lesser limitations valuable lessons about God's ability to sustain, showing them, "Brothers, think of what you were when you were called. Not many of you were wise . . . influential . . . of noble birth . . . strong" (1 Corinthians 1:26–27).

Be an invitation for others to talk about God. People who don't know Christ are curious as to why disabled people like you and me trust in and even enjoy God. And some people aren't curious at all; they scoff and think, *Handicapped people need religion.* "But God chose the foolish things of the world to shame the wise; God chose the weak things of the world to shame the strong" (1 Corinthians l:27). When you aspire to show faith, unbelievers are shamed and their puffed-up pride is deflated. Thankfully, this is exactly where God wants them to be if they are to trust Christ for themselves.

Hunger for heaven. I have written more about this in my book *Heaven ... Your Real Home,* but I will say again that people with disabilities have, more than most, a longing for "things the way they ought to be." In heaven, Christians will gain back all they have lost, and so much more. I am convinced God uses the crushing sense of loss you and I experience to lift our sights and fix our passions on heaven. Without implying that heaven can become a psychological crutch, disabilities can, in a healthy way, shatter our illusions that earth can ever really satisfy, that it can ever really keep its promises.

Present God a sacrifice of praise. God is glorified when we present to him praises wrenched out of loss and pain. If breathing is difficult for you, think of how God's heart is warmed when you sing the hymns in a worship service. If you are on disability benefits, think of the glory God receives when you tithe generously. If you are suffering from manic depression, consider the pleasure God derives from listening to your thoughtful intercessions for others.

An Eternal Weight of Glory Far Outweighs It All

QUESTION: DOES ALL THIS make a person with a disability just a utilitarian audiovisual aid in the hands of God? I think of my friend Karla Larson who has lost both legs, has had a kidney transplant, suffers from heart attacks, is almost blind and ... loves God! She inspires me so much. Is Karla nothing more than an object lesson from which others can learn? No way. What others gain from watching someone like Karla persevere through it all is being credited to Karla's eternal account.

I think this is what the apostle Paul meant when he said in Philippians 1:25–26: "Convinced of this, I know that I will remain and I will continue with all of you for your progress and joy in the faith, so that through my being with you again your joy in Christ Jesus will overflow *on account of me*" (italics mine). And listen to 2 Corinthians 1:5–6, "For just as the sufferings of Christ flow over into our lives, so also through Christ our comfort overflows. If we are distressed, it is for your comfort and salvation; if we are comforted, it is for your comfort, which produces in you patient endurance of the same sufferings we suffer."

If others benefit from Karla, God chalks it up to her account. It is a way in which someone with a disability can produce fruit in the lives of others. It is the old principle of John 15: When a disabled person remains in the Vine, the Lord will bear fruit in the lives of others through that disabled person. And as it says later on in the chapter, "This is to the Father's glory that we bear much fruit." What a weight of glory is being accrued in heaven when she decides each day that it's worth "fighting on."

This is good news for every severely disabled person who thinks her life doesn't count ... who thinks her usefulness is over ... who thinks there is no purpose for the wheelchair or the mental impairment. For God considers "Our present sufferings are not worth comparing with the glory that will be revealed in us." And what an eternal weight of glory is being amassed for Karla!

And for you too. The weight of glory may feel heavy here on earth, but, oh, how much lighter your heart feels just knowing God's got a purpose.

NINE

It's a Two-Way Street

EARLY ONE EVENING AT the Hamburger Hamlet, I was having soup and a sandwich with a friend. The tables were crowded with parents and children scarfing down quick dinners in order to catch the new Disney movie showing down the road. Across from us in the corner booth sat a little girl with her mom and older sisters. The girl wasn't eating her grilled-cheese sandwich. She had draped herself over the back of the red vinyl booth and, with finger in mouth, was staring. She was staring wide-eyed and full focused at me.

The rest of the family was busy chatting. After a couple of minutes, I decided it was time to interrupt her stare. "You think I'm pretty interesting, don't you?" I said with a sly smile.

The girl straightened. Embarrassed, she glanced over her shoulder for her mother's help. I held her attention with another question, "Would you like to know my name? It's always nice to know people's names if you're going to be interested in them."

She shook her head no.

That never daunts me. I smiled and said energetically, "Well, my name is Joni. What's yours?" By this time, the girl's mother looked around. Our eyes quickly met in an "agreement" that it was okay to pursue this educational experience with her daughter.

"Sheila," the child finally offered in a half-smile.

"Well, Sheila, do you think the way I feed myself is interesting?" I said as I lifted my paralyzed hand. She spied the leather armsplint I was wearing and the bent spoon inserted in the cuff. Her finger was back in her mouth; but she nodded a confident yes. "Would you like to ask me any questions?"

She looked at her mother, got the "okay," then slid out of the booth and ventured closer. "What happened to you?" she said, still hanging onto her finger.

"If you take that finger out of your mouth, I'll tell you ... it's a good idea to talk without fingers in the way, don't you think? Besides, they don't taste very good!"

Sheila giggled. The finger disappeared.

"I dove into shallow water. That's something, by the way, you don't want to do, do you?" The little girl was once again wide-eyed and making a mental note about swimming pools. "I hurt my neck very badly and I became paralyzed ... like this," I said, lifting my arm a bit to show her that my muscles weren't working very well.

Since I didn't want her grilled cheese to get cold, I closed our conversation. "Sheila, my story has a very happy ending because my wheelchair has brought me closer to Jesus. So remember, the next time you see somebody like me in a wheelchair, make sure to give them that pretty smile of yours when you say hi, okay?"

She jumped a little, as if to say, "This was neat," the finger went back in her mouth, and she scurried back to her booth. Sheila's mother wrapped her arm around her, pointed out the uneaten sandwich, then smiled at me and mouthed, "Thank you."

What to Do About Stares and Stupid Remarks

I CAN REMEMBER A time when I would have stared back at a child like Sheila. (I admit, though, that sometimes I still try to out-stare a kid in a good-natured game of "Who's going to blink first? Not me!") But I am not talking games. I am talking about a cold shoulder. An inability to handle an awkward situation. An "I'll show them!" way of dealing with the able-bodied world.

Why can't mothers keep their kids in line? Don't they teach manners these days? It didn't help when mothers—or for that matter, any adult—showed the same insensitivity.

"Get away from her!" a mother would hoarsely whisper, jerking her child's hand.

"I'm sorry," the maître d' would say, "we can't seat people like you in here. It would be too much of a distraction to our other patrons."

Or, speaking of manners, there was the time a woman said to me after a conference, "One day, dear, you will be normal in heaven just like us."

Long ago, I would have rolled my eyes, snapped a snide remark, or just wheeled away. But time, wisdom, God's grace, and a deep self-acceptance have changed that. As a Christian, I see every encounter—even with a child like Sheila—as a divine appointment. It's an opportunity to raise awareness, a chance to help shape a healthy attitude in another, a time to erase old prejudices and chalk up something possible on a clean slate, an occasion to make a friend.

Not every disabled person sees it this way. There are some who find it hard to put a positive spin on a sour situation. They feel it is society's responsibility to initiate change and promote awareness: "If people have rotten attitudes, phooey on them! It's their problem. Schools should be doing a better job. And so should parents. I'd love to see a TV news report on the stupid things people say. *That* would wake people up!"

Many Christians with disabilities feel it is all the church's responsibility. A friend of mine with MS was in my office not long ago to tell me about the progress her church was making toward establishing a disability ministry. I listened for one or two hopeful comments, but all I heard was a long litany of complaints. Her points were valid, but I couldn't help but think, *If I were her pastor, I'd tune her out too.* "My church is completely at fault!" she scowled.

But society is not a bunch of people way out there who sit around big tables, think up political trends, cultural drifts, or the value a community will place on a person with a disability. And the church is not a body held together by committee meetings and red tape. You and I, as disabled people, need to remember that most people are clueless as to how to relate positively toward those with handicaps. We need to remember something else: society is us. It is you. And my friend with MS needs to remember that the church is "her." She and her Christian friends are the body of Christ, which, incidentally, is not an organization but an organism.

If you want to see change, it is your actions, attitudes, and words that will help shape not only Sheila's heart but the heart of our church as well as our culture.

Change Begins with You

THIS IS WHY PEOPLE with disabilities carry the primary responsibility for initiating change. My blind friend, Jim van der Laan, says, "People with disabilities have the knowledge of what needs to be done, they have the competence to initiate change, and they have the obligation from Christ to serve and be involved." He's right. But notice the conditions: people affected by disability need *knowledge* of what must be done. Then there is *competence.* And we had better have the right *motive*—to serve Christ and others. Consider these three conditions for change.

Knowledge. I know of a mother who suddenly showed up at a primary Sunday school class and handed over her child with autism to the teacher. The little boy went haywire and the teacher had no idea what to do. He was taken out of class. A major eruption resulted between the parent and the Sunday school department. A lot of pain could have been avoided had the mother first contacted the Sunday school supervisor and arranged a meeting with the teacher to explain her child's needs. Knowledge involves understanding *what* to do and *how* to do it.

Competence. A disabled person's ability to initiate positive change may be hindered in proportion to negative personal attitudes toward himself. Dissatisfaction with your self-image breeds fear and mistrust of others; instead of thinking, *How can I help improve this situation?* you wonder, *Why doesn't this person like me?* Self-centeredness results in blaming others.

Motive. We are not out to prove a point or push forward an agenda. Our purpose is not to get "one up" on the church or show others how bumbling, stumbling, and inept they are while we, who are politically correct, come across holier-than-thou. Our motive is to exalt Christ and serve people. With Christ at the center of our motives, peace is promoted, lives are touched, and change is lasting.

Of all the things I will say in this chapter, this concept is the most important. Disabled people who are secure in Christ and see their significance in his kingdom are powerful ambassadors to initiate change in their families, churches, and communities. They aren't aggressive. They are assertive. They communicate their convictions in a positive, nonthreatening manner.

I will never forget one near run-in I had with an employee and her supervisor at the Department of Motor Vehicles. Had it been up to them, I never would have taken my driver's test. The supervisor threw one roadblock after another at me. I held my place at the front of the line and, with a smile in my voice, asserted, "I'm sure we can come up with a creative alternative here . . . something that will suit your requirements yet, at the same time, allow for my limitations." Five minutes later, the red tape had been cut and I was busy taking the exam.

Yes, at times you may need to ask for the supervisor, the manager, or the customer service department. And when the problem gets resolved, always remember to say, "Thank you"— and mean it. Disabled people must be in the business of building bridges, not throwing up more walls. Incidentally, I was at the DMV a few weeks ago to renew my license; I was pleased and impressed with the progress they have made over the years. I am convinced that people with disabilities themselves were and are behind the change—the cultural drift is shifting, the political trend is toward the positive, and the community is slowly beginning to recognize the value of people with disabilities.

We Are All Handicapped

YEAH, RIGHT!

I realize that, at first, the phrase "we all have disabilities" may seem like rubbing salt in the wound of your injury or illness. I can almost picture it. A woman at your church observes the difficult time you are having maneuvering your wheelchair through the doorway of the handicap stall in the ladies' room. In an attempt to empathize, she comments, "They make all of these restroom stalls too small. There's hardly room to hang up my purse or my coat! So," she sighs, "I guess we're *all* handicapped."

I can appreciate the woman's good-natured attempt to empathize, to identify. And she has a valid point: restroom stalls are often too small. But are we, indeed, *all* handicapped? Is it fair, with one sweeping assumption, to draw such a parallel?

Again, there was a time when words like these would grate against my nerves. In the early days of my paralysis, I would think, *No, we are not all handicapped. You don't need others to wipe your nose, dry your tears, give you a bath, or brush your teeth.* The phrase, though well intentioned, was a thoughtless platitude that only trivialized my plight.

As you would suspect, with time and a dash of biblical perspective, my view changed. From God's vantage point, we *are* all handicapped. Some limitations may be more severe than others, but God calls us to look for that common ground that binds us together and doesn't separate. The writers of the New Testament, who were facing the sword, the whip, and hungry lions in the Coliseum, wrote "Rejoice in your suffering!" Somehow I can't see them pausing with pen in hand to think, *Those guys over in Asia Minor have it easy. So what if they have to hold church from house-to-house ... so what if a couple of goats wander through their meeting! They know nothing about real persecution.* Thankfully, they didn't pause to worry whether or not they should dignify someone else's so-called suffering with their hard-won encouragements.

And so Paul wrote in 2 Corinthians 1:3–4, "Praise be to ... the Father of compassion ... who comforts us in *all* our troubles, so that we can comfort those in *any* trouble with the comfort we ourselves have received from God" (italics mine). If God pours out his compassion on us, who are we to be snippy about to whom we pass it on?

Suffering is our common ground. Affliction is the lowest common denominator for us all. We can all be humbled by hardships, whether that humility is honed through a broken neck or broken arm. And this is why I would heartily accept the well-meaning intentions of the woman in the church bathroom. To receive her words is to release the spirit of humility.

Independence or Interdependence?

FOR ME, THE LORD'S Supper is a powerful symbol. As the plate of small pieces of cracker is passed, we are ever so careful to pick up one piece without touching the others, as so many do. Our fastidious care to touch only one cracker, although tidy, seems sadly symbolic: we are careful to live our lives apart from each other, even though we are one in Christ.

I thought about this when I watched Teddy, an autistic teenager, reach toward the communion plate that was being passed down his row. His muscles twitched, his hand grabbed, and before his mother could guide him, he held up a fat fistful of bread pieces. "Teddy, no!" his mother hissed, "you're supposed to take only *one*!"

Teddy's mother was embarrassed, but I could hardly stifle the giggles. Teddy needed help and it reminded me that so did I. I am glad I am forced to depend on another Christian friend to handle my bread for me. It makes me feel connected. A part of the body. Interdependent. One with my friend. It is a happy symbol of how closely I must live my life with fellow believers.

This is exactly why I boast in my affliction and delight in the infirmity, as the Bible says to do. And I boast not only for my sake (remember, God's power rests on those who recognize their weaknesses), but I boast for Christ's sake. His body becomes stronger, healthier, and more efficient when we all express our need for one another. Christ's body is weakened when we nitpick and assert our independence from one another. "I don't need you; I can do it myself!" is not the byline for believers.

Trouble is, most Christians forget this important truth. That is, until they are pressed up against a speech-impaired girl who wants to sing in the choir or a woman in a wheelchair who desires to be immersed in baptism or a young adult with Down syndrome who wants to lead a Bible study. What appear as problems, at first, can be turned into marvelous possibilities for creative and one-of-a-kind worship; and an Emily Post, picture-perfect congregation takes on the untidy look of a church that is anything but normal and boring! It happens when Christians—especially Christians with disabilities—replace the word "independence" with "interdependence."

Interdependence becomes a blessing to the entire church as disabled people reach out to forge bonds of friendship with able-bodied people. As I said in the first chapter, you can be the person with whom an able-bodied friend feels most comfortable in sharing his struggles. You can be the person to remind someone else of the grace of God. You can help others learn how to slow down. You will help stretch the character of another, encouraging that person to see beyond his horizons, comfort zones, and discover the way God works beyond his small world.

Most of all, your disability will be the schoolroom in which others learn how to serve. I mean really serve. There is no higher calling for the Christian; Jesus himself said, "Whoever wants to become great among you must be your servant, and whoever wants to be first must be your slave—just as the Son of Man did not come to be served, but to serve, and to give his life as a ransom for many" (Matthew 20:26–28). Have you ever considered that when you "give your life" in interdependence with others, you serve "as a ransom for many"? It's true. You help ransom others out of self-centeredness or impatience. Your disability gives context to another's character development. What an honor!

Start Up a Friendship!

THIS IS EXACTLY WHAT I did the day I married Ken Tada. No, I am not suggesting that marriage is the best nor the only place to create a solid friendship. But for me, fifteen years of life together with Ken has been the most powerful proving ground for real friendship. I realize you may not be married, but remember, we are talking about principles of friendship.

Whether the friendship is expressed in or out of a marriage relationship, being a real friend is not a fifty-fifty partnership.

It's 100 percent from your end. It is what the book of Philippians is all about: "Looking out for another's interest before your own." That is the foundation of any intimate friendship. And one thing is for sure: I cannot look out for Ken's interests until I learn how to be responsible for myself.

For me, this translates into doing as much as I can for myself as I am able. After all, Ken is not my nurse, he is my husband. He has enough husbandly responsibilities on his plate without adding the pressure of ordering my medical supplies, adjusting the mechanical lift in my van, or organizing my attendant care. Besides, I can do this stuff. I *want* to do these things, whether ordering supplies over a phone, driving myself over to Agoura Auto Works, or keeping a mental chart on who comes up to the house which morning to get me up.

Even when it comes to grocery shopping—something that is not related to my disability—I like to "do it myself if I'm able." It simply means calling ahead to the supermarket's customer service department to arrange for a bag boy to give me a hand. It is just one more way I can demonstrate to Ken that I want to take responsibility for my own needs. It is also a way of showing thoughtfulness—in short, a way of strengthening friendship.

As a disabled person, you have every reason to engage another in friendship, knowing full well that you can make a difference in the life of another. By the grace of God, you can:

Talk with God about your friend's needs
Help him achieve his life goals
Give comfort through trials and sorrows
Assume responsibility for his reputation
Tell him about your faults
Be sensitive to areas in his life that need improvement
Be committed to faithfulness, loyalty, and availability
Help him be the person God wants him to be

And remember, you enter into a friendship not primarily to get your needs met but to meet the needs of another. I realize this is hard, especially with a disability. Your own handicapping condition sometimes screams for your undivided attention.

I remember being in a rainstorm with my girlfriend, and we only had one umbrella. We knew that getting soaked to the core created bigger problems for me than for her. So guess who got the lion's share of the umbrella! I felt so badly I said, "Quick! Sit on my lap with that umbrella and we'll both make it to cover!" It worked. And our friendship went a bit deeper that day, simply because my friend saw that I cared. I wish this were the case all the time, but I know I have a long way to go in all my friendships. Like you, I am still learning!

And I am learning with eight different women who, on any different morning, help get me up. It is an hour-and-a-half routine, if you throw in washing hair or changing pressure sore bandages. I don't think I'm being presumptuous when I say it's a blessing for us all. They serve God by serving me (if I have to lie back down to refix my corset, I will joke about extra jewels in the ol' crown). But I serve God by encouraging them. Between scrubbing teeth and drinking orange juice, we will sing a hymn. Somewhere before brushing out my hair, we will pray along with our JAF daily prayer list. And I can't load up in my van until my friend and I stop to enjoy the blue sky and flowering bushes outside my garage door.

That is what friends do. We minister to one another. And it feels *great*!

Your Best Friend

HOW DO YOU LIKE your friends? Do you like them to be faithful and loyal? Encouraging, thoughtful, and kind? Identifying with you at every turn? Of course you do. But how many of your friends would measure up to such standards?

Friends are people, and people are not always going to measure up to our standards. A disability is one of those factors that can either strengthen a friendship, creating openness and honesty, or it can rip apart a friendship through selfishness, manipulation, or the burden of day-to-day routine. Years ago when I was in the hospital, I learned that some people weren't meant to handle my disability—they were good jogging partners for twenty-five laps in hockey practice or great study buddies in the library, but the wheelchair skewed the equation of our friendship.

I couldn't fault them for that. True, they were no longer close or even intimate friends, but we could still be casual friends. It was just a matter of redefining our relationship. As the Bible says, "As far as it is possible with you, live in peace with all men." I had to let go of hurt feelings and simply allow people, if they chose to, to shift to a different level of commitment.

Just look at some of the people Jesus called his friends. Peter was always interrupting and telling Jesus what he should do. Then there was Mary Magdalene whose sordid past was well known. Mary, the sister of Martha, failed as a housekeeper. Indecisive Thomas never stood up for his opinions. Then there was Nicodemus, the man who came to Jesus at night, a chicken for not showing his face in the daytime.

These people had their problems. Nevertheless, Jesus valued them as friends. He didn't expect them to be perfect; he expected them to be themselves, faults and fine points together. And all he asked of them was their love. Love for him and for each other. "You are my friends if you do what I command" (John 15:14).

There will be people who will have a problem with your disability. It's a fact of life. Like Jesus said, "In this world you *will* have trouble." But don't worry. The Lord will never forsake you or leave you. He promises. And he is the Friend who "sticks closer than a brother."

What a friend we have in Jesus!

A Letter to My Friend

Dear Friend,

Someone once said, "Never confuse a memo with reality." How true. All of the ideas and suggestions in the world can't hold a candle to the reality of one moment of friendship. That's because friendships don't happen in a book. Nor do they happen in your mind. They are played out in the real world of real people.

I think you're ready for a real friendship. We've spent time seeing why friendships are a blessing to everyone involved and why they are so important for people with disabilities. The ins and outs of such friendships were described to help you step out of your comfort zone.

The true test of whether all of this will have an impact will depend upon an act of the will on your part. You have to want to do this. You have to say the word, do the deed, walk the talk. And no one can do that but you.

Are you ready for that?

Only you can answer that question, but let me encourage you with this thought. The person at the other end is ready for you. He is looking for you. She is praying that someone like you will come alongside and be a friend. So, go ahead. Make the call. Write the note. Give your smile.

It will make all the difference to them.

And to you.

Recommended Reading

Gary Chapman. *The Five Languages of Love.* Chicago: Northfield Publications, 1995.

Child Evangelism Fellowship. *CEF Vacation Bible School Curriculum.* Warrenton, Mo.: CEF Press.

Christian League for the Handicapped. *24 Ways to Help a Handicapped Friend.* Walworth: CLH, 1985.

JAF Ministries. *Disability Awareness Study Guide: Hearts in Motion.* Study guide with accompanying video or audio cassette. Agoura Hills, Calif.: JAF Ministries. (See address on next page.)

_____. *How to Create an Effective Disability Outreach in Your Church.* Agoura Hills, Calif.: JAF Ministries. (See address on next page.)

_____. *JAF Prayer Manual: Interceding for a Handicapped World.* Agoura Hills, Calif.: JAF Ministries. (See address on next page.)

_____. *Support Group Manual.* Agoura Hills, Calif.: JAF Ministries. (See address on next page.)

Robert Perske. *Circle of Friends.* Nashville: Abingdon Press, 1994.

Jim Pierson. *Just Like Everybody Else.* Cincinnati: Standard Publishing, 1993.

John Piper. *Desiring God.* Portland: Multnomah Press, 1986.

John Powell. *Why Am I Afraid to Tell You whom I Am?* Allen, Texas: Thomas More, 1995.

Herbert Simon. *Administrative Behavior.* New York: The Free Press, 1976.

Joni Eareckson Tada. *All God's Children*. Grand Rapids: Zondervan, 1993.

_____. *God's Design in a Disability*. Cassette tape, can be ordered from JAF Ministries (See address on next page.)

_____, with Joe Musser. *Joni: An Unforgettable Story*. 20th Anniversary Edition. Grand Rapids: Zondervan, 1996.

For More Information

JAF Ministries
PO Box 3333
Agoura Hills, CA 91301

http://www.jafministries.com/

About the Authors

Joni Eareckson Tada is the founder and president of Joni and Friends Ministries (JAF), an organization accelerating Christian ministry in the disability community.

A diving accident in 1967 left Mrs. Tada a quadriplegic in a wheelchair, unable to use her hands.

Mrs. Tada's role as an advocate for disabled persons led to a presidential appointment on the National Council on Disability for three and a half years, during which time the Americans with Disabilities Act became law.

Mrs. Tada serves on several boards, including the Lausanne Committee for World Evangelization as a senior associate for evangelism among disabled persons. She also serves in an advisory capacity to the American Leprosy Mission, the National Institute on Learning Disabilities, Love and Action, Youth for Christ International, and Christian Blind Mission International.

Steve Jensen serves as Director of Outreach Ministry for JAF Ministries. He cofounded the Christian Council on Persons with Disabilities and served as Executive Director for the Christian League for the Handicapped. He received his Masters in Communication from Purdue University and his B.S. and B.A. degrees from Geneva College. He is author of *The Disability Awareness Study Guide, The Great Alphabet Fight,* and *The Shortest Disciple.*

Joni

An Unforgettable Story
Joni Eareckson Tada

In 1967, Joni Eareckson Tada was paralyzed from the neck down in a diving accident. In seconds her life changed from one of vigorous activity and independence to total helplessness and dependence.

In this unforgettable autobiography, Joni reveals each step of her struggle to accept and adjust to her disability and her desperate search for the meaning of life.

Twenty years after its first publication, *Joni* has joined the ranks of the classics of Christian literature. This incredible story of a young woman who triumphed over devastating odds continues to touch countless lives worldwide with the healing message of Christ.

What others are saying about *Joni*:

". . . a remarkable portrait of Christian faith and God's grace in the face of trial and hardship."

—**Billy Graham**

"It was my pleasure to have Joni on the [Today Show] program. I shall never forget meeting her. What an inspiration."

—**Barbara Walters**

"Losing her anger at God made the difference between suicide at seventeen and a life of strong purpose. The very irony of Joni Eareckson's story suggest the existence of Someone designing destinies."

—**Mary Daniels,** *Chicago Tribune*

Heaven: Your Real Home
Joni Eareckson Tada

What Will Heaven Be Like?

Do you wish you knew more about what waits for you after this life? *Heaven* offers a refreshing and faith-filled picture of the glorious destination the Bible promises is waiting for all believers. And once you've caught a glimpse of heaven, you'll see earth in a whole new light.

"*Heaven* may be as near as next year or next week," says Joni, "so it makes good sense to spend some time here on earth thinking candid thoughts about that marvelous future reserved for us."

Heaven offers hope for the here and now, a vision that comforts those who struggle in this life. It is a vision forged in one person's faith and understanding of what the Bible has to say about heaven.

Look for *Heaven: Your Real Home*
at local Christian bookstores.

Heaven: Your Real Home
0-310-50140-7 - Hardcover
Audio Cassette - 0-310-20003-2

ZondervanPublishingHouse
Grand Rapids, Michigan
http://www.zondervan.com

A Division of HarperCollins*Publishers*

Diamonds in the Dust
366 Sparkling Devotions
Joni Eareckson Tada

Author and painter Joni Eareckson Tada opens our eyes to see glimpses of heaven on earth as she finds hope and help for life's constant challenges in this sparkling collection of daily devotionals.

With a meditation on a Bible verse or theme, a short prayer, and a thought for the day, Joni shows us where to find *Diamonds in the Dust.*

Here's a sample of what you will receive November 17:

Perspective

"They will soar on wings like eagles; they will run and not grow weary, they will walk and not be faint."—Isaiah 40:31

Birds overcome the lower law of gravity by the higher law of flight. And what is true for birds is true for the soul. Souls that soar on wings like eagles overcome the lower law of sin and death. Hannah Whitall Smith writes, "The 'law of the spirit of life in Christ Jesus' must necessarily be a higher and more dominant law than the law of sin and death; therefore, the soul that has mounted into this upper region of the life in Christ cannot fail to conquer and triumph."

Why is it then that so many Christians fail to conquer? Perhaps it's because we fail to mount up and soar with wings and choose instead to live on the same low levels as our trials. Little wonder we blunder when the battleground we choose is on an earthly plane. Christians are powerless there; that is, unless they shift to a higher battleground and choose weapons of warfare that are spiritual.

What we need is perspective. We need to see what birds see. When, like eagles, we soar on wings, trials look extraordinarily different. When viewed from their own level, trials look like impassable walls, but when viewed from above, the wall appears as a thin line, like something easily overcome.

You have wings. You don't need stronger, better ones. You don't need more wings, or larger ones. You possess all that you need to gain heavenly perspective on your trials and thereby overcome. A passive or inactive trust in the Lord won't do. To use your wings is to actively trust God.

Lord, I don't want to trust You in theory or in word only. I want my trust in You to be as active and as strenuous as "mounting up with wings." As I do, thank You for the higher, heavenly perspective You give me over my trials.

These touching devotional readings are underscored with all the hope that Joni herself has found in the most unique corners of life's daily opportunities. Available at Christians bookstores near you.

Diamonds in the Dust
0-310-37950-4 - Hardcover
0-310-37958-X - Audio Cassette

ZondervanPublishingHouse
Grand Rapids, Michigan
http://www.zondervan.com

A Division of HarperCollins*Publishers*

We want to hear from you. Please send your comments about this
book to us in care of the address below. Thank you.

ZondervanPublishingHouse
Grand Rapids, Michigan 49530
http://www.zondervan.com